# A Parson in the Vale
# of White Horse

George Woodward's Letters from
East Hendred, 1753–1761

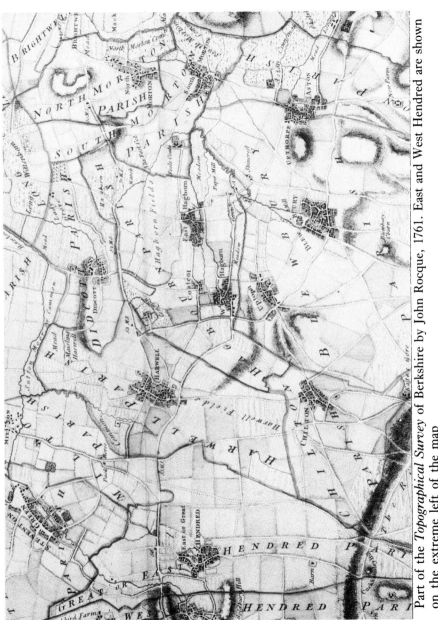

Part of the *Topographical Survey* of Berkshire by John Rocque, 1761. East and West Hendred are shown on the extreme left of the map

# A Parson in the Vale of White Horse

George Woodward's Letters from
East Hendred, 1753–1761

Edited by Donald Gibson.

Alan Sutton
1982

Alan Sutton Publishing Limited
17a Brunswick Road
Gloucester

First published 1982

**British Library Cataloguing in Publication Data**

Woodward, George
   A parson in the Vale of White Horse.
   1.  Woodward, George
   I.  Title      II.  Gibson, Donald
   283′.092′4      BX5199.W/

   ISBN 0-86299-025-4 (paper)
   ISBN 0-86299-037-8 (case)

Typesetting and origination by
Alan Sutton Publishing Limited.
Photoset Imprint 10/11.
Printed in Great Britain
by Page Bros (Norwich) Limited.

*To Shansi*

## Editorial Note

This edition is intended to entertain the general reader rather than instruct the scholar. The Woodward MSS contain 166 letters, but only ninety two are represented in the present edition, and large sections are omitted from most of the letters printed. For the serious student the originals are deposited in the Kent County Archives Office, catalogue mark U771 C7. My very best thanks are due to Mrs. Orr, owner of the documents, for her kind permission to publish them. I am also deeply grateful to the following: two personal friends, Alan Brownjohn and John McCormick, for advice and encouragement in my enterprise; Betty O'Callaghan, of the Kent Library Service, for expert bibliographical assistance; two colleagues, Mrs. K. Donne and Miss A. Wale, who very kindly undertook the typing. Several institutions provided significant help, and I must make particular acknowledgement to the Kent County Council and to the Wellcome Institute for the History of Medicine.

# Contents

## 1761

*Appendix*

Albinia Woodward to Mrs. London

## 1753

## 1755

*The rector of a parish has much to do — In the first place he must make such an agreement for tythes as may be beneficial to himself and not offensive to his patron. He must write his own sermons; and the time that remains will not be too much for his parish duties and the care and improvement of his dwelling, which he cannot be excused for making as comfortable as possible. And I do not think it of light importance that he should have attentive and conciliatory manners towards everybody, especially towards those to whom he owes his preferment.*

— *Mr. Collins in* Pride and Prejudice

## Introduction

The parsonage ranks next to the manor house as the defence and ornament of Old England. Ever since the Reformation legitimised clerical families, many of the country's most distinguished men have sprung from clerical fathers, or were themselves in Holy Orders: John Donne, William Cowper, Nelson, Jane Austen, Lord Olivier, Sir Francis Chichester, the list stretches on, one hopes, to infinity. A peculiar interest attaches therefore to the social and even domestic atmosphere which has produced such an efflorescence of talent and engaging quality of life. Something of that atmosphere may be glimpsed in the present collection of letters, written by a good-natured and conscientious country parson in the very depth of that eighteenth century which still engages perhaps our fondest, most powerful imaginings.

George Woodward was born in London in 1708, son of Richard Woodward and Rebecca his wife. Formal legal documents describe Richard Woodward as gentleman in status, but nothing more is known of him. Our George Woodward's christian name was chosen perhaps in compliment to his maternal grandfather, George London, chief gardener to Queen Anne, and father of the George London to whom the letters are addressed. This second George London was thus Woodward's uncle. He lived at Ditton in Surrey. Richard Woodward had two other sons Thomas and Charles. Of Charles the letters relate merely that he deserted his pregnant concubine and he evidently died before the period of these letters. Rebecca Woodward died young, but Richard soon remarried. His widow Mary, and her children, are major characters in the letters, and with Thomas, receive brief further notice in this introduction. Our George Woodward's childhood included stays at Ealing, now in London, and at Westerham in Kent. He was educated at Eton, and Lincoln College, Oxford. At Eton he was an exact contemporary of the elder Pitt, whom he recalls as playing at fives in the cloisters. There is no record of his employment between entry to Oxford in 1726, and the period 1732–1740, when he was a curate at Ticehurst in Sussex. The letters however refer to a fever contracted in the West Indies, and this may well date from about 1730. At Ticehurst, he met his future wife Albinia, daughter of the local squire, George Courthope. Woodward makes frequent affectionate references to Albinia, whose two surviving letters are included in this collection. The marriage was delayed till 1748, when both parties were forty years of age and sixteen years after their first acquaintance. They had only two children, both of whom lived a normal term of adult life. Woodward's late marriage therefore happily reversed the normal eighteenth century pattern of frequent childbirth and high infant mortality. The happiness of his domestic life in Berkshire imparts a slight air of enigma to the lateness of his marriage. The delay was evidently not for financial reasons. A curate might consider marriage imprudent, but Woodward became rector of East Hendred, Berkshire[1] in

1. East Hendred. Due to modern boundary changes this parish is now in Oxfordshire.

1744, and was a lecturer at the parish church in Friday Street, London, 1744–46. He spent two years alone at East Hendred, 1746–48 until his marriage to Albinia.

Immediately on arrival at East Hendred he settled into that routine of conscientious discharge of duty which is implicit in all his references to his own profession. The parish register for 1746 bears a note in his own hand that no register had been kept for twenty years till Woodward's arrival, in May 1746, but from then on the baptisms, marriages and burials of East Hendred are recorded in Woodward's own handwriting till February 1790. He died in May 1790, aged 81, having laboured for forty-four years in East Hendred, and enjoyed the income thereof for forty-six.

Woodward was conscientious indeed, but he makes no pretence to saintly self abnegation, a posture he would certainly have regarded as irrational, perhaps even highly indecent or immoral. He explicitly censures the excessive zeal of a sixteenth century divine who disdained the efforts of his uncle to make him a rich man: "the fault I find with him", writes Woodward, "is that (for the sake of instructing the ignorant) he made frequent excursions from home into a part of the north, that was inhabited by a most uncivilised set of people, that ever were heard of; this part of his character I am not very fond of".

Woodward's own professional excursions were quite different in character. The Hammonds in their *Village Labourer* draw a contrast between the windows of the French curé, which looked to the village, and the house of the English parson, which looked to the manor house. The rectory windows at East Hendred, on this view of things, looked neither to the village, nor the manor house, but to the palace, or rather two palaces, those of the Duke of Grafton, and the Bishop of Salisbury, in whom Woodward rejoiced as patrons from both the clergy and the laity of English nobility. Woodward refers to his family connection with the Duke of Grafton, but in terms which are disappointingly vague. Whatever the connection was, Woodward kept up the acquaintance with a frank self interest quite devoid of hypocrisy, or even real servility. A portrait of the Duke hung in Woodward's best parlour, a compliment which not even Mr. Collins paid to his "noble patroness". He also acknowledged the Duke's sense of humour, relating that when a political evolution displaced some friends at court "as he is not likely to be removed, he in a droll way gave an invitation to all his old friends, who were upon the move, that they might take a parting glass together". His Grace appears to have achieved an ingenious and hospitable *salon des rejetés*. "I can very well figure to myself, how His Grace behaved at the head of his resigning company upon such an occasion: I dare say he was full of his quaint speeches to them, and made them pure and merry". But even after the Duke's death there is a refreshing candour in Woodward's declaration "abstracted from all views of interest, I really loved the Duke, who was a person of an amiable behaviour towards those he was well acquainted with."

Woodward's other patron, the Bishop of Salisbury, was also his professional superior, and the Rector's attitude naturally combines reasonable professional deference with equally reasonable hopes of advancement. In 1753, relative to an episcopal visititation of his parish, "I can't say that a visitant of this rank would have given me a very extraordinary pleasure, any otherwise than I should have been in hopes, that sometime or other he might have taken it into his head, to have paid me for the trouble he had given me; so you see a little dash of self interest now and then, must go along with one's civility." Woodward also made frequent visits to Salisbury as prebend of the Cathedral, generally staying with the Bishop's brother, Mr. Gilbert, a Canon there. Naturally enough, Gilbert had one of the best houses in the Cathedral close. In the event Woodward achieved only limited success, though the Bishop did advance him to a more desirable prebend, a promotion which Woodward was pleased to regard as "further proof of his Lordship's regard for me." Woodward's most persistent hopes however were to become a fully fledged Canon of Salisbury, though he realised the Bishop's relatives would have a more cogent claim. Even their demands however could not be insatiable, and he reasons at one point "as the Bishop has now provided well for all his new relations, he may perhaps think of his friends for the next vacancies." The Bishop had no excuse for forgetting this particular friend, as Woodward displayed admirable zeal in ensuring his name was not overlooked. A canonry was vacant at Salisbury in 1757, and Woodward immediately wrote of his hopes to three incumbent canons, the Bishop of Winchester, and his old patron the Bishop of Salisbury, by now translated to York. The new Archbishop had a brother in law not averse to a canonry at Salisbury, but the appointment eventually went to a son in law of the new Bishop of that see. Woodward's anxieties, or keen interest at least, are indicated in his reaction to civilities from the Bishop and Mr. Gilbert: "I can't help thinking, by this extraordinary civility to me, that Mr. Gilbert is more apprised of my future fortunes than I am myself; else why should he take notice of me above all other common prebendaries? Why is my wife above others invited to Salisbury? What occasion is there for telling me in particular, that Canon Pile is old and can't endure long; and that Dr. Moses is ill at Bath? These are particulars, that can affect none, but those who are known to have expectations." On another occasion he disclaims excessive ambition, and a real contentment to live and die as Rector of East Hendred.

The chances of ecclesiastical preferment were of course eagerly discussed in the servants' hall at Salisbury, and Woodward learnt some of this gossip from Joe, his own servant. Woodward gathered from this quarter "I have the votes of the Lower House on my side, but whether their interest alone will be sufficient for carrying my election, I fancy is out of dispute." The greatest of poets has observed how a hierarchic but fiercely competitive society may reflect colour and interest into lives quite precluded from competition for its prizes:

> "Hear poor rogues
> Talk of court news; and we'll talk with them too,

Who loses and who wins; who's in, who's out
And take upon's the mystery of things."

Fairness now requires specific indication of Woodward's conscientious
attitude to professional duty. He very rarely censures individuals known to
himself, but one such criticism is reserved for Mr. Pennicott, parson of the
parish in which his uncle lived. Pennicott[1] was prone to over frequent
absence from his parish, and Woodward particularly regrets he did not keep
Christmas at home, and so give his neighbours "a specimen of his charity,
as well as of his hospitality." Woodward himself regarded it as a matter of
course that a clergyman should provide a deputy when himself absent from
his parish and frequently both received and performed this service. An
immoderate use of purgatives confined him to the closet all one Sunday,
and regardless of personal dignity, he sent a messenger round the parish to
cancel the morning service. By the afternoon however Woodward had
secured a neighbour to assist him, and the service was duly performed.

In 1753, he even curtailed a visit to Salisbury, the very centre of his
professional ambition, at the call of duty, hurrying back to East Hendred to
conduct a funeral. Preparing a fast day sermon engaged his efforts at some
hours, particularly creditable perhaps as he was anxious to convince his
congregations "Their main business at church is to attend to the prayers
rather than the sermon." In February 1757 he walked five miles to deputise
for an absent friend. For his practical Christian charity we may note his
contribution of half a guinea to relieve the poor in the exceptionally severe
winter, February 1757. Nor was his zeal carried to ridiculous excess. He
had intended a tour of the town to solicit further funds for the poor, but in
view of the bad weather, sent the parish churchwardens and overseers
instead.

Such was the spirit in which Woodward approached his duties. What did
he receive? On his own account a stipend of £210 from East Hendred, a
sum which presumably excluded casual fees for baptisms, marriages and
burials, and also the income from his prebendary of Salisbury. The stipend
alone was enough to make Woodward a rich man, at a time when the poor
of his neighbourhood subsisted on six shillings a week, or less than £16 a
year, assuming constant wages and employment. Goldsmith's parson was,
admittedly with irony, "passing rich on £30 a year" — one seventh of
Woodward's income. His position in the upper reaches of his profession is
confirmed in the Oxford *History of England*. "Of the 10,000 benefices in
England during the early part of the eighteenth century nearly 6,000 had
revenues of less than £50 a year", though this evil was mitigated by the
prevalence of pluralism. Even the most ample revenue however cannot be
enjoyed without some inconvenience and in this respect Woodward did not
escape the common lot of our species: "Next Monday is our farmers' tithe
feast, which is but a troublesome time, and I am always heartily glad when

1   Mr Pennicott recalls Gibbon's tutor, Philip Francis, who preferred "the pleasures of
London" to the duties of his profession.

it is over; for it's very disagreeable sitting for a half a day amongst such sort of folks, in a cloud of tobacco, attending to the price of corn and fat hogs, and almost stunned with the noise of their rustic mirth."

Besides his stipend Woodward derived significant benefits in kind from his glebe land, apparently about fifty acres, most of it let to a tenant, but a few acres at least retained for personal cultivation by the Rector and his household. Two acres of clover supplied the needs of his horse, which pulled a secondhand chaise, for Woodward made no pretence of disdain for the economic virtues. If he died tomorrow, he relates with some pride, his successor could make no demand whatsoever for dilapidations to the rectory property. In the kitchen department his ground supplied a remarkable variety of produce, the letters alluding at various times to the following: apples, apricots, asparagus, beans, broccoli, cauliflower, cider, currants, gooseberries, grapes, hens, lettuces, oranges, peaches, peas, pears, plums, strawberries and walnuts. Ducks and duck eggs were sent at times to Woodward's uncle at Ditton, and a hog slaughtered for guests of honour at East Hendred. Even this range of produce was supplemented by good natured neighbours. Woodward confessed his incapacity for field sports, but his house had a good share of game sent in by neighbours, to whom he could make no return but his obligation for their civilities. One such neighbour, Mr. Clarke of Arnton, gave Woodward leave to call him his gamekeeper. Venison counties as Woodward saw them were overstocked with proud nobility and overbearing commoners, an inconvenience from which his own neighbourhood was happily free. Nevertheless, when his friend Mr. Wymondesold enlarged a paddock for deer, Woodward hoped at some time to partake of the fruits thereof. In the event both Woodward and his Archdeacon received venison haunches. It was indeed a very easy going, above all a *neighbourly* society, where all the neighbours enjoyed a decent subsistence, and it was natural and pleasant to disburden oneself for any surplus on the estate, equally graceful to accept a like kindness from one's friends.

The combined Christian and gentlemanly ethic diffused its benefits far beyond the confines of polite society. In 1756 "Our great and good neighbour, Mr. Wymondesold, left the county yesterday morning; his parish will feel his absence, for he does a great deal of good amongst them, and employs a great many poor people: he has this and the last summer been about a very good piece of work; he has undertaken the repair and beautifying of his parish church . . . and he is now employing people about making the ways about the village better, opening a little stream that runs through it, and sloping the banks, and planting trees upon the sides of it in regular rows, which will make it a sweet pretty place; and before it was as unsightly a thing as one could look upon: these and several other such things are his constant amusements whilst he is down here, besides clothing poor people, and doing several acts of charity amongst his neighbours. A man of his disposition cannot but be of great use where he lives, and as he is a very courteous, sensible man, we think ourselves happy in such a neighbour."

There were of course serpents in this Eden, but their virulence was not excessive, and their suppression well within the powers of civilised society. Hooligans in East Hendred inflicted malicious damage in Woodward's garden, causing him some concern "at such ill usage from a parish, wherein I had always behaved as a friend to them all." He recalled however the "Black Act", passed early in the eighteenth century to deal with nocturnal poachers in the New Forest, who blacked their faces to elude detection. Mindful of the Act's provisions Woodward pinned a notice on his church door, to the effect that he forgave the criminals on this one occasion, but further offences would render them liable to death or transportation. It is pleasant to observe that Woodward's humanity and self restraint were not abused, and the letters contain no further reference to hooliganism in his garden. Surely a proper and gratifying response to Christian charity, combined of course with reasonable social discipline.

Woodward also tried to supplement his income by taking in a paying guest, but the episode constitutes his one failure recorded in the letters. In June 1759 he wrote of his plans to receive Mrs. Price of Lockinge. She was to pay £25 a year, Woodward to provide her in everything except washing. "She will be not only an agreeable person to us at all times, but also a good companion for my wife, and I fancy we shall all think ourselves the better for each other's company." She was installed at the Rectory by October of that year. In December however Woodward wrote at some length of her social deficiencies: "a very good woman, but does not contribute much to Society; for she has lived so long by her self, that she is not much cut out for a family way; somewhat formal and particular in her ways, and very ceremonious upon all occasions; no great lover of company; and not at all given to any sorts of amusements, such as cards; which is in the first place owing to her education, (for I find she has been bred among Dissenters)." By January 1760 Woodward decided to give her notice to leave his house for "we never thought before she came to us she would be so troublesome . . . Indeed she had once or twice spoke to my wife in terms, that I thought were rather fit for a common landlady, than for her."

Whatever Mrs. Price's defects, however, she at least knew a good thing when she saw it, and made repeated requests to stay in the household. She even tried to remedy her own social deficiencies "and once in the holidays sat down at a table with some young folks at whist, where they only laughed at her." Eventually she offered to "take up the worst room in the house, and raise her price, if we would suffer her to stay; I was so provoked at such a mean speech, that I could not help saying to her, that if she would offer to lay in the cellar, and give me £200 per annum I would not accept of it." She had paid for a private closet and Woodward decided therefore to forego her board for one quarter, "for I think it would be unreasonable to make her pay for what she has had so little use of, and it would not look well to the world: in short I must be contented to be a loser by my experiment of a boarder."

His household at this period consisted of himself, his wife Albinia, and two young children, also called George and Albinia. There were also three servants, one male, Joe Shepherd and two female. Joe was employed largely out of doors, and as a porter/companion on his master's travels. In 1760 he married his fellow servant in the house, Sarah, who, like himself, had worked fourteen years for Woodward. Sarah was over forty years of age, and Woodward expected no children from the union. By 1765 however he had himself recorded in his parish registers the baptisms of three children of Joe and Sarah. Shortly before the letters begin, a sister of Joe's, Molly Shepherd, had been dispatched to work for George London at Ditton, but the letters suggest she was a much less successful servant than her brother. Woodward describes her as much less good-natured than Joe. Another undermaid appears briefly in 1756, "an active, diligent and neat girl." She quickly became pregnant (not by Woodward) and was discharged with the advice to get married as soon as possible (which she did). She was replaced with a niece of the long serving Sarah, so that most of Woodward's servants were connected by ties of kinship. "Her aunt has undertaken to instruct her, who is an excellent good housewife herself; therefore we are in great hopes she'll improve under such a tutoress." Relative to trouble caused by servants, Woodward observes "it is a vexatious, though not uncommon case, particularly in and about London; it is an order of our species that we can't well do without; but there are but few of us, who have not reason to complain of them."

To the present age indeed Woodward's letters may convey a refreshing awareness that vice, folly and rapacity are not confined to the privileged orders of society. He writes in 1753 "I am very sorry to find, that the small pox is got about you again; the carelessness of the common people in this case is very unaccountable, they never seem concerned at the ill consequences of their indiscretion, especially if they find that they shall be any ways gainers by it". Following floods caused by rain he saw "some of the ragged inhabitants by the church gate, running through the rain to pull up some rails at the end of a ditch in the churchyard, to give the water a freer course, that might otherwise endanger their lousy tenements; and we observed they carried of the rails as a perquisite of their office; for firing is the cheapest article to these people, on their housekeeper's accounts, they generally have it for fetching." Woodward's view of the poor approximated perhaps to the kindly realism of his clerical contemporary, the naturalist of Selbourne. "We abound with poor;" writes Gilbert White, "*many of whom are sober and industrious.*" (Editor's italics).

Stern correction awaited the intemperate and licentious. In 1757 "We have had great riots at Abingdon this week, on the account of the dearness of corn; the mob rose and seized a large quantity of corn and flour that was on board a barge, and carried it off, in spite of the magistrates, they likewise plundered the butchers, and threatened going further; but I hear the gentlemen of the town have sent for a party of soldiers from Wallingford to suppress them . . . the necessities of the poor are great without all dispute, and there is a fault somewhere in keeping up the price of corn; but notwithstanding this, the sufferers are not to be judges of their own cause, and thus to set themselves up as redressers of the grievances they sustain; no one's property can be safe, if they are suffered to go on at this rate."

For miscreants brought before the courts confident pomp and circumstance attended the administration of justice. According to Woodward his friend Wymondesold, High Sheriff of the County "did not make so grand an appearance as was expected from a man of his great fortune." Nevertheless when he set out for the Assizes at Abingdon, he had "two French horns blowing for about an hour after dinner". Of his procession, "the High Sheriff, his chaplain, and two more friends were in his own coach; Mr. Price and his brother (two neighbouring gentlemen) were in Mr. Price's coach and four; I was with Mr. Clarke in his chariot, after which came a one horse chair with an apothecary and a country curate, followed by a squadron of horse; the horns blowed at every village through which we passed, and all sides of the road were lined with spectators of all ages."

.Such were the assizes at Abingdon. But most of the civil government of the countryside, as well as the administration of justice, was transacted by Justices of the Peace, assembled in Petty and Quarter Sessions. These sessions receive not a single mention in the letters, a fact which may be due to a peculiarity of the social structure of East Hendred. The leading local land owners, the Eyston family, were Catholics, and as such excluded from the magistracy and from public life generally. The family is of some interest in its own right, *Pace* Joseph of Arimathea, their lineage is the most distinguished possible for English Catholics, for it includes Thomas More, martyred under Henry VIII. Legend has it that mass has been said daily in the family chapel from medieval times, through periods of persecution and oppression, into the present day. Their tenacity in the faith is matched by their tenacity of the earth, for they arrived at East Hendred in the mid-fifteenth century, and show no sign of being ever dislodged from their picturesque manor house near the parish church.

Woodward also visited the assize town of Devizes in Wiltshire, "the Devizes", as he conflates the process. Never does he excuse crime by the imperfections of the social order. Twice in the letters he quotes as "infallibly true" Pope's line "whatever is, is right", though once with the important qualification "It will not hold good as to our moral concerns." Weightier evidence is provided by his choice, as his favourite sermon, that by the Bishop of Bristol on *The Division of Mankind into Rich and Poor*. "In reference to the Poor," writes the Bishop, "I would conclude that they are under strong obligations to submit to their present condition without murmur or complaint. From what hath been said, it must appear, there is no manner of reason for complaint on this head; such a portion of happiness being attainable by them, even in their lowest state, as is suitable to their condition."

We have however strayed from out test. Let us return to the rectory of East Hendred, a place as free from poverty as it was from vice and crime.

After Woodward, his wife Albinia claims pride of place. Her funeral monument describes her as "deservedly lamented by all her acquaintance for her amiable character; and by none more than her affectionate husband." The unguarded language of these letters confirms this tradition-ally charitable epitaph. There is evidence of her practical skill in the unobtrusive efficiency with which visitors were absorbed into the house, without the slightest disturbance to Woodward. One of her letters mentions that "every bed in our house was in use last week," a circumstance that is not mentioned in Woodward's own letter of the same date, 19th April 1755. She evidently had some reputation in the housewifely arts, for patients came from three or four miles around for her powders against agues. Her two surviving letters, written in a somewhat confused almost ungrammatical style, are probably inadequate witness for her intellectual capacity, though they do reflect a sound morality, as well as the natural preoccupation of her sex with the procreation of the species, and the occasional gravity-removing irregularities thereof. Her letters are published, as she, with conjugal deference would have wished, as an appendix to her husband's. Woodward himself considered his wife an invaluable complement in his intellectual and professional interests: "she amongst other great qualifications is a very good Divine; for she is a perfect mistress of the Bible and several books of divinity; which makes the reading of such books much more agreeable to me, than otherwise they would be if she was a person of no taste, and seemed quite indifferent to what I was about; but instead of that, she enters fully and wholly into the spirit of our entertainment; and by conversing together upon these sort of topics, she makes herself the best companion, as well as the best of wives." Woodward often read aloud to his wife from these "books of divinity", thus achieving with some exactness the patriarchal ideal — "He for God only, she for God in him."

Nor did Albinia display any immodest unwomanly interest in the masculine world of politics. Woodward explicitly contrasts his wife's temporary paucity of materials for a letter, with the copious field opened to his uncle and himself by the victories of Frederick the Great. Perhaps the surest indication of Albinia's role occurred when her children were innocu-lated, and both she and the servants left the rectory as a medical precaution. Woodward, left with his children in the house, described himself as "but half alive during my confinement," and a marginal note chronicles their reunion with loving precision. "N.B. We met all together on Thursday at dinner."

Woodward could hardly be expected to cope with his own meals during the temporary break up of his household, let alone the care of two children. He therefore secured the services of the blacksmith's and Clerk's wife to keep house for him — presumably the wife of the Parish Clerk, and two ladies rather than one, to avoid scandal. The temporary ménage was quite a sociable one, "very good company we are all together, for we eat and drink at one table, which makes the less trouble." Woodward appears indeed to have been well endowed with that affability which is perhaps the most indispensable attribute of his profession. The letters indicate he would readily chat to any one, Dukes, Bishops, chance acquaintances in coaches, and certainly down to the level of blacksmith and Parish Clerk.

The two young children of the rectory appear largely as objects of parental solicitude. Innoculation was a dangerous precaution against small-pox and Woodward pondered deeply before coming to a decision on the matter. His eventual decision, taken in respectful disagreement with his uncle, was prompted by a characteristic mixture of prudential and theological reasoning, "that uncommon success, that this practice meets with everywhere . . . is a method that Providence has been pleased to point out to us, for the avoiding of more danger: not that I hereby charge myself any doubts or suspicions of God's Providence and care." He sent his wife, staying at the Archdeacon's, messages three or four times a day, while these precautions were taking effect.

George went to school in Abingdon, and soon became, next to his father, the best Latin scholar in East Hendred. By 1760, aged eleven, he could read a few lines of Homer "tolerably well." In this same letter "his sister gives proof of her proficiency by a parcel of doll's caps etc. in the milliner's way; so they are both to be commended for their endeavours in their different departments of learning. Young Albinia, "Binny" as Woodward calls her, went to a Dame's school. Relative to her progress in reading "Binny makes but a slow progress yet awhile", but this was in 1755, only three years after her baptism. Also, as Woodward reasoned "there is not so great a necessity in getting girls forward in their books as boys; for they will be most of their time at home, and have but one language to learn." Woodward saw his educational scheme fully justified, for George became a clergyman like his father, and Binny a parson's wife. Young George Woodward officiated at his sister's wedding in his father's church, in 1775. We have no evidence as to whether young Binny's marriage was as successful as her mother's, but as a young girl she showed a most promising capacity for modest deference to the male. "She is a great imitator of her brother in everything, and I believe looks upon him as the finest and wisest gentleman she ever conversed with." One hopes her husband was an improvement on another of Woodward's clerical brethren. Woodward describes him as a fox hunting person "just turned twenty four and his lady a few degrees on the other side of forty, who upon several accounts may not have good reason to expect much of her husband's company, and therefore in all probability will amuse herself in her solitary chamber, by tracing out with her needle the different fortunes of the chase."

Woodward's own family enjoyed far more varied and stimulating recreation. Albinia and adult visitors were engaged in games of cribbage, and Woodward once mentions stakes of sixpence, quite high perhaps in the context of local wages of six shillings a week. This however was at the house of Woodward's rich friend Mr. Wymondesold, and was perhaps, an unusual extravagance. The main entertainment however derived from books, which Woodward read aloud to his family. On Sundays and feast days for example "I have always given them a discourse out of Stanhope upon the epistles and gospels", and in the same letter he mentions providing as variety a pamphlet "entitled Serious Advice from a Country Gentleman to his neighbours". His children at this date, were aged seven and four respectively. Woodward was also fond of historical books, particularly Clarendon's *History of the Great Rebellion*, and Guthrie's *History of England*. Nor was he intellectually fossilised among the works of the past, but enjoyed the novels of Richardson and Sterne, specimens of a virtually new form of literature which appeared during the period covered by these letters. At West Hendred too, the Archdeacon regularly read to his family for three hours at a time, from Richardson's novel *Sir Charles Grandison*, during which time no other person was allowed any part in the conversation. The novel was then locked in the master's study, till he chose to produce it again the next day. Little George Woodward showed early signs of assuming this patriarchical responsibility, for we catch a glimpse of him reading Fielding's *Tom Jones* to his sister and the servants in the kitchen.

Woodward also took newspapers three times a week, and makes frequent comments on the political topics of the day. The trials of Admiral Byng, and Lord George Sackville are recurrent themes, and on the first he anticipates the famous comment of Voltaire[1], or in Woodward's less pithy judgement "I reckon this will put mettle into all his brethren of the navy." Lord George was merely censured for inactivity as cavalry commander at the battle of Minden. It is perhaps a slight anomaly in the eighteenth century record that both these officers should have been penalised for lack of zeal, at a time when polite society showed such marked distaste for "enthusiasm."

Most of the public news however was of far less melancholy a nature, for this was the period of the Seven Years War, when the country was advancing to an early peak of imperial pre-eminence, and the church bells were perpetually ringing for British or Prussian victories. There is a particularly graphic account of how his village received the news of the capture of Louisburg, an essential preliminary to Wolfe's assault on Quebec. Woodward regularly sent the news every post night to a committee headed by the local blacksmith, "where the politicians of the village assemble and debate matters of the greatest importance to the nation: here I am informed the ministry is frequently changed, vigorous measures are concerted, armies and fleet fitted out, places are taken, and Old England appears in all her glory." On receipt of the news from Canada "the worthy members immediately rose and adjourned to the belfry, to which place I also sent them a bucket of ale, with the healths to be remembered: the whole parish was soon got together, and the bells struck up; more liquor was given by other inhabitants, and all the guns in the parish that had been employed in frightening the birds from the corn were collected together; and with these they fired in repeated volleys from the tower: in short nothing was heard almost the whole night long, but huzzas, firing of guns and ringing of bells

---

1.  That Byng was shot "to encourage the others (pour encourager les autres)".

. . . Some other village in the neighbourhood . . ., thought the town was on fire, and were coming up in great numbers to our assistance, but being better informed, retired back again, with a full resolution to have the same rejoicing the next evening." All these proceedings, as Woodward drily comments were "to the no small amusement of those, who were not inclined to sleep." The rectory at East Hendred stood directly opposite the parish church, and as he listened to that almighty clangour, Woodward may have reflected that, for the profane vulgar at least, the social discipline of his period was tempered by a perhaps excessive degree of personal freedom.

The occasion however was an important success for the British Empire, to Woodward as to his countrymen an institution of matchless propriety and splendour. Politically he was fortunate in his period of life, most fortunate in the period of these letters. Bliss was it in that dawn merely to be British, and very heaven to be a prosperous middle aged chauvinist. The unhappiness of a French education is advanced as some excuse for scalpings by American Indians, and of contact with the French generally he observes "our best orators are on the quarter deck". Much as he admired Frederick the Great, who had made so powerful a contribution to our acquisition of Canada from the French, Woodward hoped in 1761 "perhaps we shall have done with all connections upon the continent". George III's Electorate of Hanover is compared to the medieval connection with Normandy and Aquitane, "the same grand drains of all our men and money". Naturally enough Woodward's sole recorded vote was in the Tory interest, at the General Election of 1768. The letters indeed indicate an enviable confidence on virtually all matters of current interest. Dissenters and papists are regarded as blind to evidence not only from divine revelation, but also reason, or even common sense. He praises a polemical pamphlet as enough to convince a Roman Catholic writer "if one of his stamp could be convinced by sense and reason". Even the conversion of the Jews, postponed by Marvell to remotest futurity, is regarded by Woodward as not beyond the scope of a wise social policy. This was to consist of "fair and candid treatment", and "some well disposed Christians laying before them a fair and impartial statement of their case, supported by such sort of arguments, as may be thought most likely to convince them of their error." The effect of such policy is wisely left to "the co-operation of a Superior Power."

Such were Woodward's main intellectual interests at East Hendred. They were varied by visits to the outside world, regularly to Salisbury, as prebend of the Cathedral, and occasionally to the remoter regions. It is noteworthy that Woodward hardly ever stayed at an inn, his relatives almost invariably offering him accommodation. His professional visits to Salisbury usually involved an overnight stay at Penton[1] with Mr. Strother, parson of the parish and married to Albinia's sister. Oxford, Woodward's old

---

1   Properly called Penton Mewsey. About 25 miles south of East Hendred, 45 north-east of Salisbury.

university, provided both intellectual and social stimulus, and Albinia could at least enjoy the concerts and academic processions. Of the Latin orations "my wife and the rest of the female audiences were at a loss", which implies a tribute, apparently without irony, to male scholarship of the period. Even at Oxford, the honoured place of women in a patriarchal society is particularly apparent from the honours paid to Lady Pomfret "who has presented the University with a fine collection of ancient statutes, and such like curiosities." In 1756 "we had a full view of the procession that was to be made by Lady Pomfret and her retinue: about eleven it began; the doors were thrown open, and in they came with the beadles before them, the music playing a most grand march with trumpets, French horns and kettle drums; Lord Westmoreland led Lady Pomfret, Lord Litchfield and Lady Westmoreland, who were followed by several other Lords and Ladies too many to be mentioned, the nobility and gentry all dressed in their doctor's gowns, as having had those honorary degrees conferred upon them some-time before." The celebrations lasting three days, consisted of processions, orations, recitations and the conferring of honorary degrees on several gentlemen in honour of Lady Pomfret. Woodward himself wrote some Latin verse for recitation by Lord Glenorchy, but the Dean of Christchurch ordered that all such verses should be produced in his own college. "The Eton gentlemen were the crack of those two days, who did honour to my old school and the university too: as I had been a member of both, it gave me infinite joy."

Woodward took most of his meals as a guest at Corpus Christi College and characteristically adds: "the gentleman who entertained us, was Mr. Campion's tutor, and had been with [us] a week at our house last spring twelve month, so our eating and drinking cost us nothing at our inn where we lay, nor did we pay for our beds, as our horses were there; for lodgings were most monstrous dear at private houses, and at inns too, if people had no horses with them."

Every year, most commonly in the late spring, Woodward spent a few weeks divided between his stepmother's house at Axyard, London, and his uncle's at Ditton. His wife and children usually stayed at East Hendred during these annual holidays, as we may regard them, but Albinia accompanied her husband in 1756 and 1760, and young George went with his father in 1758. Woodward's progress involved a pleasing mixture of private and public transport. He drove his own chaise to Sonning, near Reading, where he left it with a farmer friend, and then caught the stage coach to London. The whole return journey, in 1759, took from 5 a.m. in London to about 6.30 p.m. in East Hendred.

London social life was on the whole uncongenial to him: "in my opinion a good basket of garden stuff is worth twenty accounts of rackets, drums and routs etc." Nevertheless, the great city provided some entertaining accounts of coronations, Lord Mayor's shows, and royal weddings, and a particularly racy story of Garrick and Kitty Fisher, the notorious courtesan. All these will be found in their place in the letters. Axyard was particularly disagreeable on account of his stepmother's taste for frenetic social activity. Some of his letters are dated from that place, and at one time he refers to the difficulty of putting his thoughts on paper, owing to a heated argument going on in the dining room; indeed "all the tongues of Babel have been let loose about my ears ever since I have been here." They complained at Axyard because Woodward allowed himself to little time in Town, yet when he did so, frustrated "my design, by filling the house with so much company, that I have but little opportunity of conversing with them except it be in public." In summer at least this social disharmony was compounded by the physical discomfort of bed bugs, though his stepmother paid £6 to rid the house of them.

Axyard lay less than two hundred yards from Aldersgate, but the elder Mrs. Woodward evidently kept pigs on the premises for in 1754 she made black puddings from one of her own, in honour of a visit from her son Jack. Even allowing for forms of civility, Woodward seems to have derived more enjoyment from staying at Ditton with his uncle. He refers on one occasion to the general congruity of their sentiments, and the general tone of the letters is one of frank confidence and a wide variety of shared interests. Best of all no doubt in these holidays was the return to East Hendred, especially when made, as in 1753, "amidst the bows and curtseys of the parish, and the ringing of bells to welcome my return."

Woodward took two holidays in 1756, the usual spring visit of about a fortnight to Axyard and Ditton and from late July to late September a tour through Kent, Sussex and Surrey, staying with his uncle and with two more of his invaluable clerical brothers in law. These were Edmund Latter, who held the livings of Bidborough in Kent and Burstow in Surrey, and George Courthope, a pluralist of Brenchley in Kent and Uckfield in Sussex. Woodward drove his own chaise, with Albinia and young George as passengers, and their servant Joe escorted them on a spare horse. Latter lived in neither of the parishes for which he was responsible, but at Southborough, a district of Tonbridge. The party made some excursions to Tunbridge Wells, where young George was taken to his first ball, and spent six pence in a toy shop. The Duke of Newcastle, recently out of office, was also at the Wells. "None of the company showed him any respect, who but a few months ago would have been pressed almost to death, by crowds of his admirers and humble suitors." As the guest of Courthope Woodward writes letters from both Brenchley and Uckfield. Perhaps this relative kept up both the parsonages there. The principal diversion at Brenchley were watching a closely fought cricket match, and a visit to Ticehurst, where the parish gave an enthusiastic welcome to their former curate. Albinia could not accompany her husband to her native parish, as the roads were too bad for their chaise, but Joe carried young George on the spare horse. The convenient "business expense" was alive and well in the eighteenth century, as is evident from a reference to the river Medway Navigation Company. With Latter, a proprietor in the Company, "we had a very handsome dinner at the expense of the Trust." At Uckfield Woodward was a dinner guest of Thomas Pelham, who eventually succeeded to the Duke of Newcastle's Sussex estate. The account of Pelham is favourable in the extreme: "courteous affability to all their company, . . . prayers constantly every night in their family . . . respected by the rich and beloved by the poor." As a crowning virtue in the Pelham household "my wife I do assure you had that respect showed to her, as to be placed the second lady at the table."

These letters, written to a close relative, naturally contain a great deal of gossip about relations and friends. It seems appropriate therefore briefly to review those who figure most prominently in the text. Following the eighteenth century deference to social rank we begin with Sir John Peachey, second baronet, M.P. for Midhurst in Sussex, and brother-in-law of the George London to whom these letters are addressed. As a member of Parliament Sir John enjoyed the privilege of franking letters, which were then delivered free of charge. He kept up a supply of franked covers to George London, who passed them on to Woodward at East Hendred. There is some evidence that but for this facility, Woodward would not have written with quite such frequency. Sir John therefore may be considered as at least the secondary begetter of these ensuing letters, but he is most often mentioned in them for his failure to beget an heir, a disability which Woodward ascribed to premature exercise of the "genial faculty." In a robust agricultural community the importance of growth and renewal was as self evident in the human as in other spheres of creation, and Sir John turned to the medical science of his day in the hope of making a personal contribution to the procreation of the species. Reviving Sir John's vigour might give incidental pleasure to Lady Peachey, but the main object was the serious public purpose of propagating the noble breed of baronets. Visits to Bath, Brighton, Buxton and Scarborough, were supplemented by electrical treatment, regarded even by some doctors as almost a universal remedy. The extremity of Sir John's painstaking self sacrifice is indicated in medical literature. Well into the nineteenth century electrical treatment for his condition consisted of direct shocks to the vital organs. Sad to relate Sir John's efforts were quite fruitless and his baronetcy pass to his brother James Peachey. Woodward once refers to James as the Groom, i.e. Groom of the Bedchamber to the Prince of Wales, later George III. James Peachey also died without direct heirs. How much happier than the Peacheys were the poor of East Hendred, whose procreative powers, Woodward assures us, were guaranteed by their simple diet of beans and barley!

The Peachey problem was inverted at West Hendred, where the Spry family included ten children. All the sons "are in a fair way of doing well", though Woodward gives particulars of only three of them. One was a Fellow of Merton College, Oxford, a post worth over £50 a year, and a younger brother was a Postmaster (student) in the same college. Another son was an apprentice apothecary in Bath. Of the daughters one was apprentice to her own sister, a milliner in London, and another kept house for her uncle in Bath. All the children as Woodward puts it, "will be obliged to go out into the world". Some hopes for their advancement were placed in Dr. Spry, who married a niece of Pitt the Elder, still more in Mrs. Spry's brother, the Bishop of Oxford. Spry himself was subject to monthly fits, which Woodward associated with the change of the moon. The two households dined with each other on their respective wedding anniversaries, and there was frequent friendly contact throughout the year.

Recurring to Woodward's relatives his attitude to his stepmother was basically that of resignation tempered with a considerable degree of respect. Her qualifications were domestic rather than intellectual, despite affectations to the contrary, and even her acknowledged virtues did not include that of frugality. "I only wish she had a little more British coin, to answer these good inclinations for doing good; a larger fortune would not be greatly misapplied I verily believe." She lived at Axyard with her daughters Charlotte, Rebecca and Ann, and Becky (Rebecca), the daughter of Tom her stepson, apparently a widower. The prospect of receiving a visit from the Axyard household filled Woodward with undisguised apprehension, which centred or perhaps was rationalised on the difficulty of washing clothes. Old Mrs. Woodward offered to pay for soap and washerwomen, but her stepson anticipated the "continual fuss and stir there would be with wet clothes, for what between the washing of our own family, and hers too . . . the house would be continually full of this sort of business . . . that article of washing was so very inconvenient, that we could not possibly comply with it, as it would keep the family in a continued scene of hurry and confusion." It is hardly surprising the projected visit seems to have been abandoned. In 1761 Mrs. Woodward moved with her daughters to Downe in Kent. She was already ill, and died a few months later. Woodward gives the news of her death, and immediately follows it with an account of the thrift he exercised in the matter of mourning clothes, and a discussion of the Lord Mayor's show, and other public matters.

He seems to have derived more enjoyment from his sisters' company. They visited Hendred occasionally, and Woodward writes of a winter visit "they make our house very agreeable at this dead season of the year; for as soon as the clock strikes seven we sit down to four handed cribbage, and play till supper time." The sisters may have passed much of their lives in a state of genteel poverty, as they expected only about £50 a year on their mother's death. Only one, Becky, made, or perhaps was able to make, any attempt to earn her own living. She became a trainee obstetrician in St. Paul's Churchyard. Charlotte seems to have been the most active and effective of the sisters, and Woodward's own favourite. He writes, evidently as a compliment "a more retired way of life would suit best with her, as she don't seem to have a genius for hurry and parade; the whole family I fancy would be much better in all respects, could they bring their minds into a more rational scheme of living." There is also the ultimate compliment "I wish she was married to a good honest parson, for she seems to be cut out for one of us." She actually died at Canterbury in 1800, still a spinster, and left whatever property she had to be divided between Woodward's own two children.

At the time of these letters Woodward had living one brother, Tom, and two half-brothers, Harry and Jack. The two latter held subaltern commissions in the army, and showed no signs of progressing beyond that rank. Their poor conditions and prospects are noted as contributing to their mother's low morale towards the end of her life.

Harry is a somewhat shadowy figure in the letters. He had at one time been in the Navy, but transferred to the army, out of envy, according to Woodward, of his brother's red coat. The exchange was free of charge, though his brother's commission cost £400. Harry left for service in the American colonies in 1754, returning only for a few months at the end of 1759. His name is associated with an early version of the Irish joke: "he seems to have little of the Irishman in him . . . for he tells them, they need be under no apprehension about him, for if he dies, he will take care to let them know it in time." Woodward considered he had an ample income, but was extravagent in hospitality and gambling. In 1761 he drew a bill on his mother for £70, which she refused to accept.

Jack's service was in Ireland, Scotland, and most of all in England, where Woodward frequently refers to him as employed on recruiting for the army. His Colonel allowed him £5 for every man accepted by the regiment, but the expenses were such that Jack like other officers, was likely to be out of pocket from the arrangement. He was however "very diligent in his profession and deserves to be taken notice of." Woodward often calls him the "noble Captain" throughout the letters, apparently as a private joke, for his promotion to First Lieutenant occurred only in 1755, and even three years later his lack of a Captain's commission was considered an impediment to marriage. Woodward found his conversation limited, "the pleasure of being conveyed from one place to another, together with the good eating and drinking that he meets with from his several landlords, appears to me to be the main of his expectations." At one time the family at Axyard were very concerned at illness contracted in Ireland, which left Jack very thin and weak. Woodward could not help laughing at the sorrowful accounts he received, as he accidentally discovered his brother had contracted venereal disease. The account continues "I intend to write to Jack before he comes home, and give him a little advice upon this matter." Whether the advice was moral or medical is not disclosed.

Jack married in 1758, and his wife seems to have created a good impression throughout the Woodward family. She spent long periods at Axyard, and her first child was born there. She died early in 1761 leaving two young children. Our last glimpse of Jack is extremely creditable. He intended making over to his sisters his share in his mother's estate.

The remaining brother, Tom, was actually some years older than Woodward. In the material sense, he was even less successful than Jack or Harry. Whereas they remained near the bottom of their profession, he had no profession whatsoever. At one time pressure of debt caused him to leave his house at Farnham in Hampshire, though he continued to live in the parish. He lived on an annuity of something over £20, and casual work "by one employment or another". At least temporarily, his annuity was made over to pay his debts. These modest resources were used to good effect: "I find he has a little cottage to himself, that he pays forty five shillings a year for, where he makes his own bed and dresses his own victuals, and seems by his talk to live quite agreeable to his own taste; so that he may be said to be as happy as any man in England". He had a daughter Becky, entrusted to his stepmother at Axyard with a promise of four guineas a year towards her maintenance, but he occasionally failed at least in punctuality of payment. A taste for drink may have contributed to his financial difficulties, but he was on the road to reform by 1757: "I believe he has left his drunken companions, and lives a good sober life; I never observed him all eager for liquor". Four years later "I am told by people of Farnham, that he does not drink in the manner he used to do sometime ago, and is well respected by the gentlemen of that place". In late middle age he had only five teeth, a severe inconvenience for one very fond of meat.

Every Christmas Tom stayed for several weeks at the Rectory, and made occasional visits throughout the year. Immediately on rising he spent some time smoking in the toilet. Like Jack, he was of only limited intellectual interests. "I can't say that either his or the Captain's company is such that I should like for a long continuance, for they are a great restraint upon my wife and I, as we cannot amuse ourselves with reading, or talking upon such sort of subjects as we usually do when we are by ourselves, because these two gentlemen have no taste for such pastimes". A distinguished party, including the Warden of All Souls College, Oxford, visited Woodward in 1755, a circumstance that prompted Tom to absent himself on two days by a visit to Abingdon fair, and then by inviting himself to dine with a young farmer. Woodward approved the wisdom of this course: "to speak the truth I did not much care to show them such an uncouth relation of mine."

Woodward's last significant relative was his uncle, George London, to whom the letters are addressed. London's father, as gardener to Queen Anne, had clearly reached the top of his profession, and in other respects was something of a Samuel Smiles in his generation. In his will, made in 1713, he advised his son to "stick to his trade, and proceed in it with care and diligence, and not by any means decline because bequeathed enough to live on, but that both together may be the best means to advance him in the world." At least for the period of these letters the son seems to have completely disregarded this salutary advice and lived the life of a rentier on the estate bequeathed him by his father. The fault, if any, was perhaps not entirely his, for he "was not bred to one of the learned professions." Some residual influence of the eminent gardener may be traced in that both he and his nephew seem unusually interested in their own gardens. Woodward himself considered his uncle's vineyard the finest in England. London seems to have passed some of his time in writing theological essays, which perhaps from mere civility, received high praise from Woodward. It seems unlikely that any were published, for none survive in the British Library. Woodward also frequently condoles with his uncle over the latter's long engagement in a law suit, extremely vexatious and expensive, but never referred to as a serious threat to London's position in society. One letter refers to London's teaching English to a Frenchman, though there is no evidence that he persisted in the undertaking. Woodward's comment on the attempt is one of casual but characteristic chauvinism: the diffusion of London's integrity among the French, as well as his native language, would be of great service to both kingdoms.

The letters are clearly part of an incomplete series, with no indication as to what has determined the incidence of survival. There was evidently no estrangement between the relatives. When London died in 1770, he left Woodward a reversionary interest in his house and furniture, the interest being contingent on the death of Mrs. London. There were no children of London's own marriage, though at least one step daughter, Mrs. Croft.

A very few facts are available for the rest of Woodward's life. In 1764 he succeeded his brother in law George Strother, as rector of Penton Mewsey. Barbara Strother was patron of the living. Another Strother, Catherine, presented young George Woodward to the parish of Grateley in 1773. Albinia died in 1780, and her husband recorded her burial without comment in the parish register of East Hendred. He died himself in 1790, some thirty years after the period of activity, prosperity and apparent happiness recorded in the letters.

Now read on.

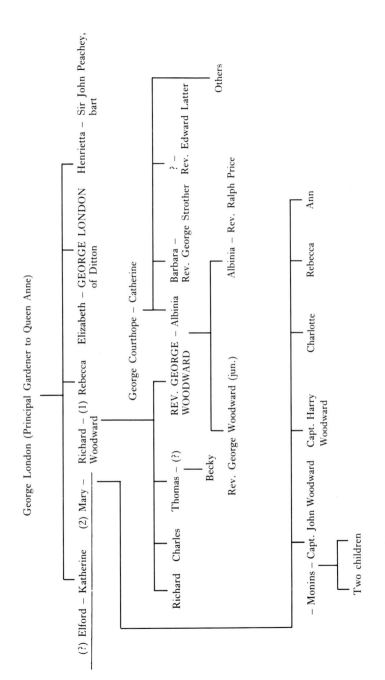

*Family Tree of the Rev. George Woodward of East Hendred, Berkshire, and his uncle, George London, of Ditton, Surrey*

Jan 13 1753

Dear Sir,

About the time I had the favour of yours I got rid of my cold, my eyes now being perfectly well again; but I find it is a complaint that several People have been subject to this winter. The weather is now very much changed for the worse, frost I like much, but take no pleasure in Wind & Storm, which we have had much of within these few days last past; I once was fond of windy rocking nights, and could sleep the better for them; but I can't say they agree with me now, they generally put me into great disorder & flutter of spirits, last night was very stormy, and I had not a wink of sleep till almost three o'clock, which has no good effect upon me today, as you perhaps may find before this paper is out: whether it be owing to my being more fearful than I used to be when I was younger (as I know I be in several other respects) or whether it be, that I am now possessed of Something of my own, that may possibly be injured by these turbulences I know not; but I am always very much out of sorts upon these occasions; tiles and thatch are things that Storms and tempests have a natural antipathy to; and as I am now more obliged than I used to be to stand by them and see they come to no damage.

I find by the news-papers that several people have showed a great aversion to the alteration of the style, particularly with regard to the observation of Christmas day; I think they could not well have made more disturbance if the day had been entirely abrogated by Act of Parliament:[1] it's to very little purpose to pretend to set such obstinate people right, in this or any thing else; but it is evident enough, that upon the true principles of astronomy, we have been wrong for some hundred years last past in our observation of that day, and (if there is any thing at all in the particularity of the day of the month, which I think there is not) the Gregorian Calculation, which we now have complied with, is most certainly the newest: but the common people don't like it, because it has something to popery in it they say; I wish we had no other reason but such as this to find fault with the Church of Rome: some folks in my parish have been fools enough to give their servants and cattle a holiday upon the old Christmas day; who I supposed observ'd the festival, as they usually do on most country places, by getting heartily drunk; the parish in general came to Church and the sacrament upon the new day; but not being satisfied with this, the old day (as I said before) was observed too, as far as ringing of bells and arousing is thought to be a proper celebration of it: but I hope by this time twelvemonth they'll grow a little wiser, and not be carried away with such a zeal without knowledge.

I forgot to mention one thing, whilst I was talking about Xmas, which makes some talk in this neighbourhood; a man at Milton about 2 miles off,

---

1   Chesterfield's Act to reform the calendar. It provoked the famous London riots: "Give us back our eleven days".

having observed the great zeal of the Vulgar about keeping of Christmas, and the no small stir that was made for the ascertaining of the right day, thought he might make some advantage by the general superstition, that prevailed amongst them; he had observed what talk there was of the Glastonbury Thorn,[2] which by flowering upon Xmas morning and going off again at night was supposed to be the proper standard, whereby people might judge of the day: he therefore gave out that he had a flower in his garden that was of the same nature with this wonderful thorn, and it would accordingly make its appearance very early upon old Xmas day and close again at night: numbers of people got together at the time, to see the opening of the flower, but none were admitted under a penny a piece; when they were all come with their candles and lanthorns, he raised the ground with his finger, and showed them the flower just opening, which was satisfaction enough to them; their business would not give them leave to see the whole progress of the day; so away they went fully convinced, that that was the right day; the man, they say got about ten shillings by his stratagem; for it appears since that he had raised it under a beehive to satisfy the credulity of these people.

My paper being now at an end, I must beg you and my aunt to receive of my duty, and to present the same together with my wife's to Lady Peachey when you see her next; and we are very glad to hear that the young lady is so finely recovered from her late indisposition, and I hope she'll now live to make Sir John a happy father in due time. I think Mr. Croft is in a ticklish situation just at this time, by the account you give of him; but I hope every thing will at last succeed to his wishes, and that he will meet with more success in town than he was likely to do in the country:

I am dear Sir your dutiful nephew
and obedient humble servant

G. Woodward

N.B. Writing bad, being just before candlelight.

Hendred Feb. 3rd 1753

Dear Sir,

Since I wrote to you last I have heard from my mother that my brother Tom has been in Axyard, and has informed her that his affairs are so much out of order, that he must be obliged to leave his habitation; and she has been so kind as to take his child under her care: I have heard nothing from him myself, but my advice would be for him to go to sea, and make over his

---

2  According to legend, Joseph of Arimathea brought a staff from the Holy Land, and planted it at Glastonbury in Somerset. It grew into a thorn tree which blossomed only at Christmas.

annuity to his creditors, till his debts are satisfied, which would be a means of his doing justice to them, and beginning the world again with more courage and alacrity; for if his debts amount to about 40 pounds, as I think she told me, his annuity will more than discharge them in two years, and then by what will remain out of it (supposing he saves nothing at sea of his pay, as I imagine he will not) he will be enabled to begin again, and with good management to go on with some comfort: I am sorry for his misfortunes, and should be glad if I could assist him otherwise, but by my advice.

My wife is at present out of order with a cold, that has settled in her teeth, but I hope it will not trouble her long; the two little ones are pure and well, and both improve every day in every thing they are capable of; George is at my elbow, and wants to write something to his uncle and aunt, but as he is not able to do that himself, I believe I must do it for him, but assuring you and my aunt, that he and his sister join with my wife and I in our duty to you both.

February 1753

Dear Sir,

I am very obliged to you, Sir for your kind wishes with regard to my patron, the Bishop of Sarum; he is a man not to be solicited too much, and I have heard him say, that he would never do anything the sooner for being asked; and seems to be one who would have this merit to go along with his favours, that they were a free gift; a proper address to him, whenever I fall in his way, is the utmost I must pretend to; any thing beyond this would mar all my expectations, and be very inconsistent with the policies of that court. The weather being now more open, and the faculties of my mind being a little more enlarged, which have so long been benumbed and frozen up by the winter season, I must begin to fix upon my subject for the Bishop's entertainment at the ensuing Visitation. With regard to our family affairs, which you mention, I think Sir you are very kind in considering my brother Tom's little girl in the manner you propose, which to be sure will be an easement to my mother, and what she handsomely acknowledges: I believe (as you do) that Tom is in the main very honest, and I hope he'll find out some way or other to make his circumstances more easy; my thoughts upon the subject you have had before. As to my aunt Elford's family, I never knew so much of them before, and do think they have acted very imprudent parts; but when people will not attend to the advice of their friends, and those who are supposed to know better, their sufferings must be charged to their own account; your reflection is just enough in general, that people are apt to indulge a lazy indisposition, when they depend so much upon the aid and assistance of others; and I am apt to think, it is better in the main for people to have no such good prospects at all; for then they are under a necessity to exert themselves with vigour; which is often the means of bringing to light some secret qualities that recommend them to the favour of the world; which otherwise might have lain hid and concealed, and been for ever buried in indolence and inactivity. I shall write to my mother by this post, and shall take care to acquaint her with the particulars you mention, that regard this branch of our family. We are glad to hear that Molly Shepherd is likely to please you and my aunt, I hope she'll always endeavour so to do in every thing, she has a bad mouth, that's the truth of it, but I fancy you'll find nothing come of it worse than rotten teeth, and such things as them are better out than in: Now I am talking about teeth, I am desired by my wife to let you know, that hers are now very well again, and that she has no more cause for that pain than Molly Shepherd has.

Hendred March 3rd 1753

Dear Sir,

I am very sorry to find, that the small pox is got about you again; the carelessness of common people in this case is very unaccountable; they never seem concerned at the ill consequences of their indiscretion, especially if they find that they shall be any ways gainers by it. We at present stand clear of this distemper, how long we may be free from it I know not; for there is a house (though at a good distance from the town) which takes in people to nurse; there is one from Little Hendred down with it there now; but as they have had several of late in the same condition, and the infection has not got up to us, I hope too we shall escape it at this time.

I believe it won't be very long before I shall have the pleasure of seeing you at Ditton; for by a letter I had this week from Town, my mother wants me to come up and wait upon my great friends as she calls them, to let them see that I am alive, and I believe another reason may be, she is in some doubt whether she can come down here this summer: and as this is the case, I think of going from here the day after Lady Day; I intended indeed to have waited upon you and my aunt sometime in the summer; but as I am now to be in Town so soon, I shall pay my duty to you from thence: I think of being absent three weeks, half of which I shall (with your leave) spend at Ditton; but of this you'll hear more before that time.

Sunday Night
April 1753

Dear Sir,

According to your orders I am set down, to give you the history of that part of my life that has past since the civilities I received at Ditton; I know that I should disoblige you and my aunt, if I was to say so much as I willingly would upon that subject, therefore I must satisfy myself with having barely mentioned it, and proceed to my history. My stage coach companions from

Dear Sr.                    Sunday night.
          April 1753

According to yr. orders I am sett down, to
give you the History of that part of my Life, that
has past since the Civilities I rec'd. at Ditton; I know
that I sh'd. disoblige you & my Aunt, if I was to say
so much as I willingly w'd. upon that subject, therefore
I must satisfie my self with having barely mention'd
it, & proceed to my History. My Stage=Coach
Companions from Richmond were a Grandmother,
& Mother, & two Grand=Children; the least of 'em
was about 7 months old, & if it had not been
disappointed of its afternoon's nap, w'd. have been
pretty company, but the poor thing did nothing
but cry most part of ye Way: I thought Mr. &
Mrs. Croft were too far behind us to overtake
us; but just as we got upon Westm'r. Bridge,
they came up to us, & after a civil Salute at
a distance we parted. When I came to Oxford,
I found my Broth'r. & all ye family just as I had
left 'em, only there had been some further Prepara-
=tions for Harry, who was to go on board o' Friday,
in order to sail ye next day. On Wednesday morning

Specimen of Woodward's handwriting, describing his companions in a
stage-coach

*(Kent Archives Office)*

Richmond were a grandmother, a mother and two grandchildren; the least
of them was about seven months old, and if it had not been disappointed of
its afternoon's nap, would have been pretty company, but the poor thing
did nothing but cry most part of the way: I thought Mr. and Mrs. Croft
were too far behind us to overtake us, but just as we got upon Westminster
Bridge, they came up to us, and after a civil salute at a distance we parted.
When I came to Axyard, I found my mother and all the family just as I had
left them, only there had been some sudden preparations for Harry, who
was to go on board o' Friday, in order to sail the next day. On Wednesday
morning I set out in a hack upon my formal visits; the first was to Miss
Peachey's, whom I found at home (though Miss Becky was preparing for
church, and went away just as I did) I believed my aunt's letter, which they
did not read whilst I was there, they were very glad to hear you and my
aunt were well, and upon my giving them an account of Lady Peachey's
illness, they concluded to go and pay her a visit some day this week, though
they seemed to think it would be a little inconvenient, because they could
not have the use of Mr. Peachey's post chaise, he being to set out for
Windsor this week: they told me, that they were in company with Sir John
and Lady Peachey, and Mr. Peachey and Lady Caroline the night before,
and upon saying that I had been with them, they expressed themselves in
very civil terms, and that they should be glad to see me too, when I had
finished my visit here. I drove away to Dover Street, but was obliged to
leave my name at the door, Sir John and Lady Peachey being both from
home: and as Miss Peachey told me, their brother Mr. Peachey was hardly
ever to be met with till between one and two, being a great walker in a
morning, I didn't go there at all, but proceeded to the Duke of Grafton's,
where after I had been sometime, I put the case again to his Grace about
Windsor, who made this answer to me, *Well, we'll see what can be done for
you;* upon which I made a short speech proper to the occasion, and with a
low bow retired to my chair; and after sitting sometime got up and took my
leave, his Grace wishing me a good journey into the country. I then waited
upon the Bishop of Sarum, and told him what I had done, and the answer
his Grace had made, who smiling said he wished me good luck, but was
afraid I should meet with great difficulties; I then put his Lordship in mind
of his visit here at Hendred, who thanked me very kindly, but said he could
not positively conclude upon it yet, but if he should give me that trouble,
he would let me know of it; so after a little common discourse about
indifferent things, and a gentleman coming in upon business, I took my
leave, and drove home to my Mother's. The rest of my time in Town was
spent in buying some mourning for myself and my wife; from whom I
found a letter as soon as I come to Town: and on Friday morning I and the
gentlewoman and her daughter who is now here, set out in the stage for
Reading, together with a country attorney and a Parish clerk; we all agreed
very well together; and as to the last of my fellow travellers, I should not
have known his calling, but by some suspicions I had of him from his habit,
and a particular church tone he had in saying Amen after Grace; as this

somewhat heightened my suspicions, I had them afterwards positively confirmed, upon his offering to assist me with putting on my great coat; for he then took an opportunity of telling me, that it was what he was very much accustomed to, *not only coats Sir* (says he) *but gowns and surplices too, for the Dean of Carlisle,* who is Rector of a church in Reading; as I have some knowledge of the Dean, I desired my compliments by this worthy member of the church. The next morning my female companions and I set out for Hendred, where we arrived between two and three; my wife and her companion, together with a neighbouring clergyman, whom I found at our house, come out about a mile to meet us, but returned back again upon not seeing us; and afterwards we come into Town, and met with Sarah and the two children, whom we took into the chaise and proceeded in this manner to our own house, amidst the bows and curtseys of the parish, and the ringing of the bells, to welcome my return. I found my wife and the little girl pure and well, but poor George is much out of order with a cold, which I hope won't continue long: we have had another person die with the smallpox, since I was absent, (an old man, and a great drunkard) he was buried the night before I came home, and that was the reason of this clergyman's being here that I mentioned above. I think this is all the news, that I can pick up for you at present.

Hendred May 5th 1753

Dear Sir,

I am very glad to find that all your fears of the small pox have been so ill grounded, and that you are under no apprehensions of its making its appearance amongst you again: I hope too, that we are clear of it in our neighbourhood; there having been more taken ill since the death of the last person, who was buried the night before I came home. I have had a difficult matter to get rid of my cold, that I brought to town with me sometime ago; for I have been very much out of order with it, since I came home; but as I have been bleeded and purged, I think I have at last got the better of it; my wife too and both of the children have been greatly indisposed with the same complaint, but I thank God they are all now got pretty well again; George being but a flimsy spark, has lost some of his flesh by it, but as he is now pure and well, and eats and drinks heartily, we hope he'll fetch it up again. I never heard of his Grace of Grafton's disappointment in a bishopric for his friend before; but I hope (as you do) that he may have interest enough for a canonry, if he will but push for it; but I know his Grace full well, and that he will want to be pushed a little himself; but this I must trust to; I have done what I could towards it, the next must be left to another hand, in things of this nature I am so much a friend to myself, and my own peace of mind, that I never choose to give much encouragement to my expectations; for as I don't love disappointments, I keep my hopes at a distance, notwithstanding they sometimes would push themselves upon me,

and lay claim to an intimacy that they never had. There are two great
preferments, besides the two vacancies at Windsor, which are now in his
Majesty's disposal; one of them is given away, I am told already; that is a
canonry of Christchurch, which has been vacant about a fortnight; the
other is a prebend of Durham, which I hear is intended for a son of Lord
Albemarle's; and who are to have the stalls at Windsor, is not yet determined, if one should fall to my lot, I shall not be displeased, and if it does
not, I shall not be disappointed,: so much for Philosophy, founded upon
the expectations of a Berkshire parson. My female visitors, who came down
with me from London, stayed almost a fortnight with us; they returned
yesterday was se'nnight; and highly pleased they have been with our
situation in life, and the entertainment they met with, for I think we lived
chiefly upon hogs' flesh, happening to kill a hog the Monday after they came
here, which was the most acceptable thing to them, that we could give
them; our garden too furnished them with Broccoli and asparagus, which
they were highly delighted with: as they have been old acquaintance both of
mine and my wife's, and were no strangers to the former scenes of my life,
it was no small pleasure to them, to see the alterations that I had made in
the drama, and the several persons and characters I had introduced into the
play, that is now acting for the benefit of the author. As to my wife's legacy,
it is just what I thought it would be, £100: but Mr. Campion, who was my
aunt's executor, has been so kind, as to give us £20 for mourning, and he
writes me word, that the legacy, together with the £20 will be paid to us
about half a year hence. Before I received yours I had a letter from my
mother who seemed to be in a peck of troubles, about not hearing of my
aunt's coming to Town, as she expected and (as you observe) had conjured
up in her mind some sickness in the family, which is generally the first
monster, that makes its appearance to a very sanguine constitution, and is
supposed to be the only thing, that can possibly baulk their expectations of
seeing a friend; for my own part, this is generally my last suggestion, for I
dont love to make the worst conjecture, when a better perhaps may serve
my turn as well: I could not get a categorical answer about coming to
Hendred this summer, but something that approached very near to it, for I
find the hopes of seeing my brother Jack from Ireland are very strong, and
pretty well founded, and if that should be the case, her journey will be laid
aside; and another thing I happened to mention put a visible check upon
the scheme in hand; and that was the article of washing at home for so
many, which I told her we could not possibly undertake to do; for though
she offered to hire washerwomen, and pay for the soap; yet coals (especially
with us) is a very great article, and what it was impossible (I told her) to
know how to charge to the account; besides the continual fuss and stir there
would be with wet clothes, for what between the washing of our own
family, and hers too, which could not possibly be at the same time, the
house would be continually full of this sort of business; I told her we should
be very glad of her and my sister's company down here, upon reasonable
terms; but that article of washing was so very inconvenient, that we could

not possibly comply with it, as it would keep the family in a continued scene of hurry and confusion, and by that means deprive us of the pleasure, we should otherwise enjoy from their being here. This sort of talk, I found, was not quite pleasing to her, so she told me that she should be very glad to come down and spend the summer with us, for she longed to see the little ones, and had in a manner set her heart upon it; but as there were so many objections in her way, she believed she must make herself easy about it: I replied, that I hoped she didn't think, that I throwed all this in her way, because I would not have her come; but as she was pleased to give me leave to propose the terms, and that they should be such, as would by no means be prejudicial to me and my wife, I hoped she would not take it ill that I excepted against the article of washing, which she must know would be the cause of great trouble and confusion in such a house as ours, even supposing she provided every thing at her own expense: so at parting she told me she should consider of it, but was afraid she should not be able to compose her design, and put it upon Jack's coming to England: but I fancy, whether he comes or not, we shall not see her here, and indeed I can't say that I much wish for it, purely because I know we should have but little enjoyment, when the family is so large, and made up of two sort of servants: I own I should be heartily glad if I could with conveniency comply with her inclinations, because she has (I am confident) a great love for me and mine; and as she poor woman has met with great disappointments, and cutting afflictions in life, I should be pleased to contribute such a small matter as this if it lay in my power, to make her happy.

Hendred May 26 1753

Dear Sir,

I don't hear that we are to have the honour of a visit from his Lordship of Sarum as I was in hopes we should; I have had notice from his apparitor of our Visitation at Abingdon, which is to be next Friday; but as I have heard nothing more from his Lordship I suppose his route lays some other way; I can't say, that a visitant of this rank would have given me a very extraordinary pleasure, any otherwise than that I should have been in hopes, that sometime or other he might have taken it into his head, to have paid me for the trouble he had given me; so you see a little dash of self interest now and then, must go along with one's civility, it is not well to be supported at all times without it. We have been very much engaged for 3 or 4 days last past, with bricklayers and carpenters; for I have been repairing the steps at the foregate, which wanted it enough, and patching up holes about the chancel, with some other odd jobs of that sort; and we are now putting up a little pallisade upon a wall at the end of the garden, which looks out upon the road, it being at the bottom of a slope planted with flowering shrubs, which you perhaps may remember to have seen the beginnings of when you were here last summer; so that I think we shall look very smart this summer; for our garden I think will be in greater perfection than ever it was; as for renunculas's, I believe there are few, who can show so fine a border of them, as we have at present under the wall on each side of the foregate, just in view of the lobby window, which you know is our summer apartment. My wife has taken up her pen, to see if she can scratch out a letter for my aunt, and as we suppose our two little brats will take up a good part of her paper, as they frequently do that of our time and thoughts, I shall not rob her of a favourite topic, by entertaining you with anything relating to them.

Hendred June 21st 1753

Dear Sir,

I thought I would not let this parcel go without a line or two from the parson of the parish, though he has nothing very material to say, having wrote to you so lately as Saturday last: but it was well that I took my pen in hand then, for since that time to this day I should not have been able to have done it, having been extremely ill with the cholic; on Friday evening I found myself a little out of order with some twinges and gripings in my bowels, upon which I had recourse, as usual to a piece of rhubarb, which operated very well; but whether I caught any cold at that time I know not, but on Sunday morning about two o'clock I waked in violent pain, and was obliged to get up to the close stool; but had no relief there; I then took some pepper mint water, and after some time that took effect, and brought it to a violent purging, which continued all that day; I was obliged in the morning to send round the parish to give notice there would be no service till the afternoon, (though it was a Sacrament Day) and then got a neighbour to assist me: the Archdeacon and Mrs. Spry came over in the afternoon to see how I did, and they advised me to take a dose of tincture of rhubarb that night, which I did, so that I was upon the stool good part of Monday again; on Tuesday morning I waked early with another motion, attended with somewhat of piles, which made me very weak and low; my wife would have me send for our Dr. Cooper, which I did, and he prescribed some proper things for me, which I took yesterday, and now think myself fine and well, though I have not been out of doors, nor hardly down stairs till today, since Saturday; tomorrow I am to take some physic, and that is to be the finishing stroke. I don't know, that I ever was so much out of order before, except when I was ill in the West Indies, for I have had a lurking fever about me all this while, which is now got the better of: today I am to eat some chicken, for I have had nothing yet but milk porridge and water gruel, which is but sorry diet for me, who have a tolerable good stroke at a joint of meat.

As we have kept our strawberry beds well watered this dry season, we have large quantities of them, and very fine ones, particularly wood strawberries, which are the largest I ever saw; we sent a large parcel to Mrs. Eyston the other day, which was an agreeable present, as she had none herself by the neglect of her gardener, and particularly as she happened that day to have some company come down from London to visit her. I see by last night's papers, that two of my Reverend brethren have given offence by their preachments against the naturalisation bill; I reckon the Jews will now become a common topic, and furnish out a great deal of curious matter both for poetry and divinity; they must expect to meet with sallies of wit from every quarter, and stand the arrows of Grubstreet as well as the batteries of the pulpit: though I must own this will be no right way of proceeding, if we have any thoughts of making a conversion: I think a fair and candid treatment of them would be much more likely to have a proper effect upon them; and I don't at all doubt, but we shall every now and then see some well disposed Christians, doing their best endeavours towards so good a work, by laying before them a fair and impartial state of their case, supported by such sort of arguments, as may be thought most likely to convince them of their error: we have persons among us, of the laity as well as the clergy, who are capable enough of giving them these charitable assistances, and I dare say such will be tendered to them; but what effect they will have, must depend upon their own disposition, and the co-operation of a Superior Power.

Hendred Sep. 29th 1753

Dear Sir,

I am glad to hear the grapes are likely to be so good this season; I can't brag much of ours, and indeed we have not many to brag of; but I don't know how it is, we never have any that comes to any sort of perfection; I fancy our soil is not kindly enough for this or any other fruit; we are too much upon a cold white earth, and as soon as the roots get in to that, the trees never thrive as they should do, and the fruit has not its proper flavour. I find you have been a great dealer in venison this summer; I should have been glad to have been one of your company; but that is a rare sight in our parts; for we have no parks in our neighbourhood, and I am so unfortunate as not to have one venison friend to my back: my great neighbour Wymondesold is now enlarging a paddock, and intends to stock it with deer; so that we are in hopes sometime hence to partake of the fruits of it: there is one inconvenience, that often attends a great venison county; it is generally over stocked with proud nobility and over bearing commoners; and as we are without these sore plagues in our neighbourhood, I can very well dispense with the rent of venison, and rest contented with Ilsley mutton. I wonder much at the rude behaviour of the young Hertfordshire squire, who seems to be setting out into the world with no very good grace; it is a very troublesome as well as an unthankful office, to be any ways concerned with the affairs of a headstrong young heir, whose education in general as well as their giddy season of life in particular, renders them very untoward, and altogether insensible of advice for their better conduct; every thing that is proposed to them for their advantage, if it happens to run counter to their own fiery inclinations, is looked upon as an affront to their manhood, and most bitter infringement of their natural rights and liberties. I must return you my thanks for what you are pleased to say, with regard to our little boy; as to the management of his diet, we have in some measure been beforehand with you, for his drink is most generally toast and water and barley water; and I have for some time past restrained him as much as I could from malt liquor, which I can't say he is particularly fond of; as to his eating, pudding is his general diet, more by choice than by any thing else; and I shall endeavour, as much as I can, to keep him to such sort of diet as you direct: his present disorder indeed is owing to the measles, which he had sometime ago, which together with a cold he had caught, has made him hold his head very much towards one shoulder; this too has been attended with a low fever, which we have almost got the better of by the use of the bark;[1] and we find now that he gets his head more upright than it was about four or five days ago; but by some complaints he sometimes makes we are apprehensive he has some imposthume gathering about his ear, which we hope will discharge itself that way; he is for the most part pretty brisk, and his appetite is very good, so that we hope he is much better than he has been: I intend to give him asses' milk, in order to recover his strength, for these disorders, which he has had so immediately upon the back of each other, has very much weakened him to what he was about three weeks ago.

Oct. 21 1753

Dear Sir,

Towards the conclusion of your last you seem to think that my Salisbury expedition will furnish out a packet instead of a letter, as I am always desirous of giving you the last entertainment, that I can pick up, I shall endeavour for that purpose to make my letter as long as I can, by giving you the history of my self and my two companions, from the day of our setting out to the day of our return to Hendred: a day or two before we were to set out, old Mrs. Eyston was taken ill, and a physician from Oxford was sent for, who gave them but little hopes of her life; for that chronical distemper of eighty one is too stubborn for the rules of physic, and baffles the skill of all the faculty: the condition of the old lady did somewhat embarrass me with regard to my intended journey; for though I did not visit her in her sickness, I was not willing to be absent at the time I might be wanted to perform the last office of humanity for her, because I thought it would not be so respectful to the family (though they be Catholics) to leave the interment of her to another person; therefore I wrote a letter to her son, and let him know that as the physician gave them no hopes of her getting over this illness, it might possibly happen, that I should be wanted during

1   Quinine.

my absence from Hendred to perform the duty of my function for her; and as I was sorry I was under a necessity of being from home at this juncture, I had given orders at home to be sent for, as soon as the day was fixed for her funeral, (if it should so happen whilst I was away) and I should be obliged to him, if he would give our family as early notice of it as he could. This letter I sent the Wednesday evening, and wished heartily that she would but hold up till about Monday or Tuesday in the week after, for then I should be at home on the Friday, (that is yesterday) which would be time enough to bury her; with these hopes and wishes we set forward on Thursday morning between eight and nine for Penton; the weather had been wet for two days before, which made it but indifferent travelling, and that day itself was very windy and great signs of rain almost all the way; but we had the good luck to escape that and every other disaster, and get safe to Penton about six in the evening: when we had got within four or five miles of Penton, the road was thronged with horse and foot, and carriages of all sorts, returning from Way Hill fair, which was then just begun; and as this was a fair so remarkable, and what we had never seen, we thought we should have some pleasure in being present at it, it being kept but half a mile from my brother Strother's house: the next morning proved wet, or else we had walked up to it before dinner; but just as we sat down to dinner, a letter was brought in to me (that came by somebody to Wayhill Fair) from Mr. Eyston, to acquaint me that his mother died the evening before, and that as I was at so great a distance, they did not propose burying her till Tuesday: this was but an unwelcome piece of news, for I must now be put in such a hurry, that I should have but little enjoyment with my friends, so I wrote an answer to it, that I should be sure to be at home by that day, and carried the letter up in the afternoon to Wayhill, and sent it by a man of Wantage that I met there, who was to be at home the next day: This you see Sir was Friday, the next day by six o'clock in the morning away I went for Salisbury; but when I came there I found my Bishop was gone to Bath; his brother (who is one of the canons, and expresses great civilities to me at all times) told me his Lordship was very well, but he thought the Bath waters might be of service to him after a fit of the gout, which he had the latter end of last summer; this gentleman had one of the best houses of all the canons, extreme good rooms in it, with all the offices very convenient about it, and a handsome large garden behind, with a stream at the bottom of it; whether it was from my appearing very much in love with the situation, or from any other cause I know not, but the day after, in the Cathedral, as he and I were sitting together, our stalls joining to each other, he said thus to me — *I should be glad Mr. Woodward, to see you have a better seat in this church; and I believe I shall, whenever there's an opening made:* I own what he said gave me a secret pleasure, and it seemed to me as if he had some good grounds for so saying, or else he would not have expressed himself, I think, in such sort of terms: all the answer I made to it was, that I was much obliged to him for his good wishes, and I should think myself happy in being a nearer neighbour to him

than I was at present. As I was obliged to set out for Hendred on Tuesday
morning early, I had not much time to spend at Salisbury; so as soon as I
had dined I got off, and came to Penton that evening; the next day was wet,
so we stayed within doors; and Tuesday about seven I set out (leaving my
wife and sister behind) and got home at two; as soon as I had dined, and
dressed myself I went to Mrs. Eyston's, where the undertaker new dressed
me again in a silk scarf, hatband and gloves, and the next morning Mr.
Eyston's servant came to me with his master's compliments, who desired I
would accept of a guinea instead of a ring; and thus ended the last business
with the old lady: our people at home here tell me, that as soon as she was
dead, all the Catholics in the town were summoned together, and to chapel
they went, to say Mass for her soul: the funeral was very private, she was
carried by six of the tenants, followed by her eldest son and daughter, the
servants and tenants. The day after I came home, Joe returned again to
Penton with the horses, in order to bring my wife and sister home; where
they arrived yesterday in the evening safe and sound. I am promised the life
of Archbishop Tillotson to read in a little time, which I shall be very glad to
see, for by the account I fancy it will be very entertaining; it was lent to my
neighbour Archdeacon Spry, and as soon as Mrs. Spry has done with it, I
am to have it; she has it at home at present to amuse her, whilst her
husband is at Oxford, who is there with two of his daughters, who are just
now under innoculation for for the small pox; it was their own urgent
desire, which the Archdeacon complied with, because, as they will be
obliged to go out into the world, and particularly to Bath, where one of
them is intended very soon to be her brother's house keeper, he thought it
would be more agreeable and safe for them, to have that bad distemper well
over, before they went to a place, that is so liable to infection; they were
innoculated last Tuesday sennight, they began to be out of order on
Monday last, but how it is with them now, I have not yet heard. Mrs. Spry
was to have a letter from thence last night: I heartily wish them well, and
can't but pity poor Mrs. Spry, who is at home by herself, with these two
girls at Oxford under this operation, whom she dares not visit, and two
little boys at Abingdon now down with the measles: but I hope some few
days will carry off all her fears, and give her something better in exchange.
I imagined before you saw him, that my brother Jack would not be very
lavish of his observations, that he made in his travels into Berks and
Oxfordshire; for his curiosity seems to be little more than that of a stage
coachman, who can seldom give an account of anything more, than the
goodness or badness of the roads, and the names of the inns that he passes
by or stops at; Jack seems to have no taste for any of those things, that the
generality of people look upon as curious and worth their observation: the
pleasure of being conveyed from one place to another, together with the
good eating and drinking that he meets with from his several landlords,
appears to me to be the main of his expectations, in the excursions he makes
from home: as to what you say, of his appearing a little sick of his post, I
think I observed the same in him whilst he was here, which I am sorry for;

but he must now make the best of a bad market; I would never say anything to discourage him, but rather the reverse. Our little boy is got pure and well, and begins to pick up his crumbs apace; I hope we shall be able to regulate him in his diet, as he ought to be, for he is very well satisfied with toast and water: but I believe Sir you a little misrepresent my affection for him, by fancying that he is too much indulged; for I do assure you he is not, either in eating or drinking, or in anything else that may be prejudicial to him hereafter, either in point of health or education.

Jan. 26 1754
Saturday morn:

Dear Sir,
The Wednesday after I wrote to you, my brother Tom came in, just as we were dressing to go to dinner at Mrs. Eystons; it being a frost when he set out from home, he chose to walk, but the thaw coming on before the first night, he had but bad travelling the rest of his way: he cleaned himself up, and went with us to dinner; and whilst he was with us, we had three or four more places to dine at, where he was very well entertained with Christmas fare; he proposed going back again on a Monday, after he had been here about ten days, but as the weather was bad, I advised him to stay till the Friday after; because Mrs. Eyston was to dine with us on Tuesday, and Thursday we were invited to our neighbour the Archdeacon's; and the next day (I told him) he should have our horse to carry him to Reading, which should be brought back the next day by a higler of our parish: this proposal was in no way disagreeable; so on Friday was sennight he set out for Reading with one of the Archdeacon's sons, who was going up to Town in the stage: whilst he was here, he behaved very well; was very regular with regard to his pipe, which he always took to as soon as he was up in the morning, the first place he went to, after he was dressed, was the Temple of Cloacina, where with the tube levelled in a horizontal posture from his mouth, he performed his sacrifice to the invisible deity; for it is agreed (I think) by all ritualists, that next to the exhortations from her own subterraneous altars, the goddess is most pleased with the fume of this grateful weed. I find, by discoursing with him, that another year will set him clear again in the world, for his annuity is made over for the discharge of his debts; at present he hires a room, and by one employment or another gets enough to support him, till he has paid his creditors: he seemed desirous of some good book (as he called it) so I gave him Taylor's Holy Living and Dying; and upon talking to him upon the subject of religion, I found he had never been at the sacrament; so together with some advice upon that head, I gave him a plain instruction upon this part of his duty, written by the Bishop of Sodor and Man, which I thought might bring him better acquaintance with this ordinance; with these books and a guinea in his pocket we parted, but I have not yet heard how he got home, though I suppose it won't be long first. And now I am upon the subject of brother-

Hendred House, East Hendred, owned by the Eystons, a leading Catholic family, since the mid-fifteenth century. There was frequent friendly contact between the Eyston and Woodward households

hood, I must say, that I am of the same opinion with you, with regard to my brother Captain; I think he will not well brook his next voyage to Ireland: I hear he is engaged pretty much this winter in balls and dancing, which are scenes that will naturally come full upon his mind, just at the time that he is going to leave them, for others of a less agreeable nature. The Salisbury preferment, which you mention, I saw; but as it was not a canonry, it did not much engross my thoughts; my views are there and there only; this was only a prebend, though perhaps a better than I have myself; but no one ever has two of these at a time; I am much obliged to you Sir and both my aunts, for having me in your thoughts upon the occasion; and sometime or other I hope you'll hear some news of this sort, that we shall all be pleased with. We have the pleasure to hear, that my brother Strotter's two girls are both well recovered of the small pox, they have had it very light, the youngest in particular (who was innoculated from her sister) has had but very few, and those not likely to make any marks: my sisters, who are with me, desire their compliments to your self and my aunt; and indeed they make our house very agreeable at this dead season of the year; for as soon as the clock strikes seven we sit down to four handed cribbage, and play till supper time; the rest of the day is spent in working and reading.

Saturday Feb. 16 1754

Dear Sir,

I hope this letter will find you in your garden, looking over the ravages and devastation of the late hard frost; and giving some necessary directions to William and Thomas, who I suppose are very busy in preparing the beds, and assisting Nature in all her future productions. Business of this sort is going forward here at Hendred; for we have suffered greatly in our broccoli, and cauliflowers; we perhaps may have some side shoots from the former, but the latter are entirely cut off, together with most of our lettuces: but we hope, by the help of a hot bed that is now made, we shall get these things in pretty good forwardness. The frost has not only damaged our vegetables, but it has demolished a mud wall in the garden, that I repaired but last year; so that I must now be obliged to build it all up new; and as there is a house in the neighbourhood going to be pulled down, I intend to buy some of the bricks, in order for this purpose, which will be better and cheaper, than having new ones: the wind too, which we lately had, has uncovered another wall in the farm yard, so that all that must be new thatched: you see what it is to be troubled with old buildings, and so much of them, they are a constant charge every year. We have great complaints about us for greens, and I suppose you are not better off in your parts of the country; bacon is but poor stuff without cabbage; but our farmers and poor people are forced to get it down now without it; some of them indeed have a few parsnips, but they are but scarce, and now and then

they bake apples and eat them with it, which they say does very well; I was
told that parsnips were sold at Reading for three pence a piece the week
before last. I think verily this frost has been as severe, for the time it lasted,
as that about fourteen years ago: I suppose you have not been better off
with colds than we have; myself and my two sisters have fared the best, but
the rest have all been very bad with them, particularly my wife and the two
children. Now and then indeed one of my sisters and George and I took a
little walk out in the fields, but this was not repeated very often: I had one
walk, which was a very good long one, about fourteen miles there and home
again; this was to a funeral where I was invited to hold up the pall of an old
lady of eighty five, who was my namesake; I never saw her but once, but
she had given directions how she would be buried, and amongst other
things named four clergymen to hold up the pall, and I being her namesake
was pitched upon for one; we had scarf, hatband and gloves; it was a very
private funeral, for nobody was invited but us four, the apothecary who
attended her in her illness, and the clergyman who buried her, and both
them had scarf, hat band and gloves as we had; eight men were appointed
to carry her to church, which was about a mile and a half from the house,
who had no gloves or hatbands, but half a crown a piece; the Sunday after a
sermon was preached for her, and sixty four people had each of them a
twelvepenny loaf; when we came to the house where she died, there was a
piece of cold roast beef, with beer and ale, white wine and red, all which
she had been so particular as to order upon the occasion, before she died: I
understand she was a gentlewoman of no great fortune; she was aunt to a
dissenting gentleman of a very great estate in our neighbourhood, and had
lived a widow there above sixty years. I took a walk the day before
yesterday to my neighbour the Archdeacon's, where I found them all in
high raptures with Sir Charles Grandison, which they had just got from a
friend at Oxford; and we are to succeed them in the reading of him as soon
as they have finished a volume: when I came home I thought to surprise my
wife and sisters with a story I had made up for them; but my wife found me
out before I had got half way: they asked me, as soon as I came in how they
all did, which I answered, but at the same time said they have got a vast
deal of company come to their house from Oxford; what, says my wife, I
suppose the cousin that they have expected so long; no, says I, not her
neither can I well say who it is, for I did not see them, they were not come
down stairs; they came there last Monday in three vehicles, but were so
complaisant as to send the servants and horses back again (for three
volumes came you must know by the carrier), they have something
particular in them, for they never made their appearance, till five in the
afternoon, (the Archdeacon you must understand never beginning to read
them till that time, and then only three hours) and then they all come down
into the parlour; but what is very odd, nobody but the Archdeacon is
allowed to bear a part in the conversation, the rest sit by as hearers only,
and they all say they never were better entertained; as soon as they have
done talking, which is never longer than eight o'clock, they all retire again

to their chambers, and are seen no more till the same time the next day: (for the Archdeacon locks them up in his study, that nobody shall forestall the market:) this account was too extraordinary not to be seen through; so I was soon detected in my story.

Hendred March 16 1754

Dear Sir,

I am glad to hear that your law suit is so near a conclusion; as to the charges attending it, these are grievances most justly complained of, but I believe will never be redressed; for Justice is a mercenary deity. The story you tell us of Lady Kingston's sister and the German count is strange enough but not uncommon; I have some little knowledge of a lady of a much larger fortune, who narrowly escaped a match of the same sort; he was not indeed a German count, but he was a genteel Irishman, and I have given him many a shilling when he was servant to a friend of mine: the lady's brother whom you mention to have had this mishap, I have some knowledge of; he is a Fellow of All Souls College though I believe not that brother who was concerned in this affair, who I suppose was an elder one. I don't know whether you may have heard any thing particular from Axyard of late; if you have not, it perhaps may [be] best not to say any thing of it to them, till they mention it themselves; but I understand my brother Harry is lately returned there, by no means an agreeable visit! What was his reason for so doing I am not yet acquainted with, but am told I shall soon hear, when my mother's spirits are a little better, which at present are not very good, both upon this account and that of parting with my brother Jack, who set out for Ireland last Monday morning: I hear he is come home with the relics of the Scotch distemper about him, (and is under an apothecary's care for it) which he caught in his visit to some friends in Edinburgh, if those may be called friends who confer such favours as these upon their visitors.

Hendred May 4th 1754

Dear Sir,

I had the favour of yours by my newspaper, and am glad to hear you and my aunt are well. Sir John (I see by the same) had a tight struggle; but I am glad he has carried his point, if it be only for our own private interest; there's not much of public spirit in this sentiment of mine own, but there's a great deal of truth in it, and that perhaps may do my business as well. I told you in my last, that my wife's sisters were to leave us the Wednesday in Easter week, which they did accordingly; but I could not prevail upon them to excuse my acceptance of a very handsome present, by way of acknowledgement (as they were pleased to call it) of the trouble they had given us; which was to the value of ten guineas: I would feign have not had them been so bountiful to us, for the obligation before was on our side, as they were so kind as to make the dead season of the year pass away so agreeably; and as to trouble, they are the most easy people that can be, nor did their being with us make any great alteration in the expenses of the house; but it is the nature of the whole family to be very generous, and at the same time to be very obstinate, when they have such points as these to carry: I waited upon them as far as Hungerford, which was half way to Penton, where my brother Strother's machine took them up; and we have since heard that they got well to his house. We are to have some more visits this summer out of Kent and Sussex: on Wednesday next we expect my brother and sister Latter, who live within two miles of Tunbridge Wells; they propose spending a week with us, and then pay their visit at Penton: and sometime here we are to see my brother and sister Courthop, who have never been here or at Penton yet, but whether they have yet fixed upon their time of coming, we can't tell: so that you see, if there be any happiness in the mutual intercourse of friends and relations, that have a value for each other, (as I think there is a great deal) we have our share of it. You ask me what my neighbour the Archdeacon says to our expositions? He very much approves of them, and thinks the account very rational; at present indeed his thoughts are engaged upon a very different subject, the subject of innoculation, having his four youngest children now under that operation; it is supposed the distemper will make its appearance next Tuesday or Wednesday; I hope they'll all do well, as indeed there is less danger to be apprehended in children, than in grown persons; and if they all do well, I think the Archdeacon and Mrs. Spry may look upon themselves as very happy people, in having such a fatal distemper so well over with ten children, six of whom will then have it by innoculation: the family this week have been in a great deal of hurry and confusion; for it was Tuesday morning the children were innoculated; and as it was done in their own house, Mrs. Spry and the Archdeacon with some others were to remove to another house, in the neighbourhood; so there was great bustle in carrying things backwards and forwards; just in this interim comes a letter to give them notice of the death of her brother's wife, Dr. Hume, a resident of St. Paul's, who was to be brought down there to be buried this week; so there was another flutteration; the next post gave them notice that a vault was to be made, and the corpse would be there on Thursday by two o'clock; so to work the men went about the vault, worked all night and had not finished when the hearse was at the church gate; I was sent to over night to bury the corpse; when I came to the house there was Mrs. Spry all in hurry and confusion about the number of people, that were to be there at dinner, and what we should do about providing enough for them, and how we should dispose of them all in the little house they were got into; so I bid them send away immediately to our house for a joint of meat, which stood them in good stead at the time; and as to dining, some were to be entertained down at their own house, and some in the little house they were in, and the horses to be put into the stable and barn as well as they could; so in short they had in all to eat with them that day sixty people, besides their own family: about six o'clock they all dispersed, and left them to recover themselves of the hurry and fatigue of that busy day: I had a very handsome scarf, hat band and gloves given me upon the occasion. But all this happening just at the juncture of the innoculation, occasioned great uneasiness and flutter of spirits; and Mrs. Spry is one who is not fit for sudden emergencies. We have a large old house between us and the Archdeacon's, that is now pulling down, and the materials all to be sold; so I have been a purchaser for some old oaken wainscot, which I intend to up chair high in our little parlour, where the paper is torn and wore away; it stands me in eightpence a yard, which I think is cheap enough; I have also bought some stones at 5 shillings a waggon load, to repair my mud wall, that fell down in the garden last winter; so that I think I shall now put it up again in such a manner, as will be likely to stand longer than my time: I wish this house had been pulled down eight years ago, I should then have covered my walls with wainscot instead of paper, for there is a great deal of it, and very good for that purpose, and cheaper than paper; besides other materials, that I should have found use for at that time.

Hendred June 21st 1754

Dear Sir,

What you say with regard to children, and the great anxiety they frequently bring upon their parents is true enough, and may be a good reason for those to comfort themselves, who have none belonging to them; but those who have, should turn their eyes upon the brighter side, where children are well disposed, and by their early conduct and behaviour prove themselves to be (what they are undoubtedly intended) real comforts and blessings to their parents; my neighbour the Archdeacon seems to be a very happy man in this respect; out of ten children three are in the world with reputation, three others are grown up, and are sensible well disposed young folks, and the four youngest seem to promise as well. My brother and sister Courthop talk as if they should not be here till sometime in August so that if I can be sure of this, I intend to come up to Town by the stage, which now goes just by our town, and make out a fortnight between Ditton and Axyard; and as we propose going into Sussex next Summer, my wife will defer her visit till then. You ask me how provisions are with us? They are very dear, particularly butchers' meat; but this is an article that don't concern us, we now have the advantage of our butcher; for I agree for three pence a pound all the year round, take what meat and what joints I please; so that present we are upon a better lay than some of our neighbours: but I hear beef is 3½, mutton, veal and lamb 4d a pound: but though you are so badly off in point of provisions, we have as much reason to complain of the dearness of firing, which is a great article; wood we use but little, and that now is dearer by 6 shillings a load than it was two years ago; but coals is the worst of all things we have to do with: we can't help ourselves, I think, so it's not worth while to be uneasy at it. I have now finished my wall at last, that I have before mentioned, and it's a strong piece of work, and I dare say my successor will thank me for it; but I have an ugly stroke of thatching to do before the winter, when I can get straw enough; for the old barns are always wanting something or other to be done. I hope our farmers will all get rich this year, for there is great prospects of plenty of all sorts of grain; I think the crops in general look finer than ever I saw them. I am sorry to hear Lady Peachey is in such a declining way, I hope she is in no great pain; for all that we can wish our friends, when they are going off by age and infirmities, is that they may go off easily. What you say of Sir John is very commendable: I hope the Scarborough waters will set him up strong again for many years. If the weather holds fine, we propose to make our hay this next week; we have very large grass, and it's what I expected, for we were very good husbandmen this winter, in laying out a good deal of manure upon the field, which I hope will pay us for our trouble; they talk of hay being very dear, for though there is a prospect of great crops, yet there is none left of last year's hay: I reckon your hay harvest about you is almost over by this time; your own land, if I mistake not, is laid down with grass; so I suppose you have done. The natural genius of the schoolboy begins to open and expand itself apace in little George; it shows itself this year in the knowledge of birds and their nests; he comes home from school, and gives us long accounts of what nests such a boy found, and how many eggs were in it; and that such a boy found a sparrow's nest with six young ones and squabled them, which is a term here signifying, that he killed them all; he hardly ever goes by a hedge, but he is sprung into it, and trying to climb the trees; but he has already learnt to show favour to the martins; and robins, which he knows I won't have disturbed being a breach of the laws of hospitality; so they are safe; but as to sparrows and starlings, which we have abundance of, they are all under a severe persecution, being very prejudicial to the farmers: but though these are his amusements at home about the house and garden, together with wheeling away the grass and weeds in his barrow, yet I must say for his credit, that he minds his books, and comes on very prettily; he is now in his psalter, and reads about ten verses in the psalms for a lesson tolerably well; he takes great delight in spelling, and we often make it a diversion among ourselves to spell every word that we speak to one another, which helps to improve him in an easy way. But I must not forget my little girl, who don't yet pretend to know many letters; but she is a great imitator of her brother in everything, and I believe looks upon him as the wisest, and finest gentleman she ever conversed with; she can drive a wheelbarrow, and go a hop, step and jump too as well as him, and listens much to all his wonderful stories of birds nests; her tongue runs from morning to night about one thing or other; and what pleases me most of all, is, to see the sweet disposition of these two little creatures, for they are both very good tempered children, and extremely fond of one another; and George being the eldest always humours her in every thing; which shows a great deal of good nature, and something of good sense as far as such a little fellow is able to show it.

Hendred, July 13th 1754

Dear Sir,

In a post or two after I wrote to you last, I had a letter from my brother Courthop, wherein he tells me, that we were to see him and my sister here as soon as their hay harvest was over, which was then just begun; I immediately answered it, and desired him to give me notice as early as he could, of the day he intended to be at Hendred, for then I would send my man to Wallingford to meet him; but though I have been in expectation of a letter from him every post, I have heard nothing from him yet, and it is now three weeks since he began to cut his grass; but as it has been showery weather, it perhaps may be longer in hand than usual. We are at present under some apprehensions, that we shall be visited by the small pox, before the summer is out, for it is now spreading itself through the whole town of Wantage; which is a great inconvenience to us here at Hendred, because we can't well do without a frequent communication with that place; it is also very much at Oxford, but I don't find it prevented great numbers of people making their appearance there last week; where there were grand doings in the theatre as a compliment to Lord Westmoreland their new High Steward, as perhaps you may have seen by the public papers: if the small pox had not been there, I should have treated my wife with one oratorio; but as I could not have her with me, I stayed at home with her: for an amusement at this time, we had a book which was just then lent us, called the life of Bernard Gilpin, who was a famous divine at the very beginning of the Reformation; if you have not read it, it perhaps may entertain you; 'tis a small octavo; and I think agreeable enough: he seems to have been a very good man, but of a more squeamish conscience than the clergy appear to be nowadays: his old uncle Cuthbert Tunstall[1] Bishop of Durham would feign have made him a rich man; but he would not let him; he might have several good warm preferments, if he could have dispensed with pluralities: he had one living of £400 per annum; with which he made a very great figure, and did most surprising things, for he is supposed to be a very great economist, and at the same time a very generous man: the fault I find with him is, that (for the sake of instructing the ignorant) he made frequent excursions from home into a part of the north that was inhabited by the most uncivilised set of people that ever were heard of; this part of his character I am not very fond of. My wife and I last Sunday drank yours and my aunt's health in a particular manner with many wishes for your mutual happiness; for (if we don't mistake) we had set it down as your wedding day: ours comes on Tuesday next, and then (as usual) we are to have the Archdeacon, Mrs.

---

1   Cuthbert Tunstall: Bishop of Durham 1530–1561.

Spry, and two of their daughters to dine with us; we generally return the compliment to them upon old Twelfth Day; they are two grand festivals in the Hendred Calendar. I sometime ago was under some concern for poor Jack, who is in Ireland; for by a letter from him, and others from Axyard I understood he had been very ill, and was got very thin and weak; but within this month I could not help laughing to my self at the many sorrowful accounts I have had of him from Axyard, my mother speaking of him in a most lamentable strain, and my sisters in their letters calling him poor thing, and saying that he had not yet quite recovered his illness, and how he was obliged to march twenty miles through the rain in such a weak condition; I say I could not help laughing at all this, since by a most unlucky mistake of the noble Captain's, I had a letter directed to me (which cost me thirteenpence) that was intended for an intimate friend of his in Town; wherein I found the whole account of his late indisposition, that gives so much concern to the pitiful family in Axyard; the whole matter is the Captain, in the ardour of his heart attacked a fort and won it, but unluckily received a shot in the groin, which he is not quite recovered of: this is a secret, that I must desire may rest with you, Sir, for none of the family know anything of it; but as he is to be in England in October it was thought necessary for him to apprise them of his illness, that they need not much wonder at his looks, when he comes home: the letter that came to me I sent to his friend, with some few strictures upon it; I intend to write to Jack before he comes home, and give him a little advice upon this matter.

Hendred July 28th 1754

Dear Sir,

If you have had the same heavy rains in your parts, as we have had here within these last ten days, I reckon you are sensible of the effects of them; for they have lodged a good deal of corn about us, especially the barley, and it has been a great hindrance to the hay harvest; I wish it mayn't spoil a great deal of hay, for the natural grass is now in the midst of its making; that part of our town at the east end of the church was all in a flood last Friday sennight, and the water poured down the slopes in the garden, and out of the fore court gate like a torrent, I don't know any body that was pleased with the sight, except our two younkers, who were vastly delighted; particularly when they saw some of the ragged inhabitants by the church gate, running through the rain to pull up some rails at the end of a ditch in the church yard, to give the water a freer course, that might otherwise endanger their lousy tenement; and we observed they carried off the rails as a perquisite of their office; for firing is the cheapest article to these people, in their housekeeper's accounts, they generally have it for fetching. The County Assizes were held last week at Abingdon, where a good for nothing farmer (to the great discredit of the parish of East Hendred) was con-demned to die for cow stealing; the fellow for several years held the honest occupation of a miller, and was supposed to have picked up a few pounds in that employment; and upon the strength of this enrolled himself with the order of farmers; but not being able to carry on his business in this new profession, without the assistance of those arts, which throve so well with him in his former employment, he unfortunately over reached himself, and was caught in the noose at last: as the halter generally cancels all debts, I must be contented to have mine of about fifty shillings, wiped off with the rest of my neighbours by the same sponge.

The small pox still spreads among the people at Wantage, and I am afraid it will go through the whole town; at present indeed few besides children have it, and it seems to be a favourable sort, as it generally is at first breaking out; I hope we may have the good luck to escape it here at Hendred: at present indeed we are under apprehensions of the hooping cough, which is much amongst the children in the town, our two little ones I believe must have it, for they have both coughs, and great symptons that it will turn to the hooping cough.

Hendred September 28 1754

Dear Sir,

I returned from Salisbury yesterday was sennight, and found all well at home, his Lordship was much as I expected to find him, after a severe fit of the gout, and at that time troubled with the gravel; however, I dined with him Saturday and Sunday; nothing passed that gave me more expectations than I had before; but as I was returning back to Panton on Sunday evening, where I had left my wife, Joe was entertaining me (as he often does when we travel alone together) with matters of intelligence, that he had picked up in the servants' hall; from whence I am informed that the gentlemen of that board talk much of a removal from Salisbury to London or Winchester, whichever becomes vacant first; but I am apt to think this advice is a little premature, for I have been told these vacancies are to be filled by Oxford and Peterborough: amongst other things it was reported from that Honourable Society, that the Revd. Mr. W...... d was to have the next canonry that became vacant; this was a matter of great joy to their worthy brother, who I found could not be very easy till he had emptied his mouth to me; I told him that I had no reason to wish it not true, but I was afraid that there was no other foundation for such a report but their good wishes to me and civilities to him; however, be that as it would, I charged him not to talk of it; because if it should come round to the Bishop's ear, that I had published such expectations as these, it would be the most ready way to have them disappointed; for it would be time enough to rejoice, when we could mention it with greater hopes of succeeding in our wishes. You see Sir, by this account, that I have the votes of the Lower House on my side, but whether their interest alone will be sufficient for my carrying my election, I fancy is out of dispute: I was willing to make you acquainted even with the shadow of my expectations, for whether there can be any real foundation for such a report, I can't be able to say, though it is not impossible, but some of them may at some time or other have heard a word dropt in conversation at his Lordship's table which might be a reason for their saying what they did: but be it as it will, I think it is best not to say any thing about it, nor to build much upon such slender hopes, if the thing does come to pass, it will be welcome news; if not, I may then say, I was not greatly disappointed. The Bishop's brother and I are very great together, he wants me to make a little longer stay with them, when I come there, that we may spend a little more time together; for I did not see him for above half an hour on Sunday morning before church at his own house, except at dinner the two days with the Bishop, and I can't help but say I like him extremely, for he is a free easy good natured man, and a man of good sense, so I believe I shall spend a little more time with him the next time I go to Salisbury.

I think we have been very lucky in having such a fine season for our journey, for it made it extremely pleasant; all the way we went we had a blue sky over our heads and not too hot, with fine bowling roads through the midst of the harvest fields, that were all alive with the people at their several labours: we met with partridges in abundance at the tables we were at, but no venison, except one fine haunch at his Lordship's palace; my brother Strother made us a present of a brace of birds, that we brought home with us: and in talking with him about books for our winter's entertainment, he was so kind as to lend us Stackhouse's History of the Bible in two volumes folio, which I packed up in my great coat, and tied upon the cloak bag behind the chaise, so this will hold us for some time; we have just made a beginning, by going through the Introduction, which is a judicious performance and very entertaining to my wife as well as my self, for (to let you a little into her character) she amongst other great qualifications is a very good Divine; for she is a perfect mistress of the Bible and several books of divinity; which makes the reading of such books much more agreeable to me, than otherwise they would be if she was a person of no taste, and seemed quite indifferent to what I was about; but instead of that, she enters fully and wholly into the spirit of our entertainment; and by conversing together upon these sort of topics, she makes herself the best companion, as well as the best of wives.

The small pox still continues very much at Wantage, but I don't find that it gets any nearer to us; they are now innoculating as fast as they can, so I am in hopes all will have it who are to have it, and then we shall be a little more at ease; and as the winter is now coming on, we perhaps may escape the infection here. I believe there never was known so fine a season for the harvest, our parish have all done this week, and they have great plenty of all sorts of grain; so if the farmers don't grow rich, they are not likely to be in great want; my tenant has no less than eight ricks in the yard, besides the barn full; so that as soon as they get to thrashing, I must go to work with some of the straw, for I have a great stroke of thatching to do before the winter. I had a letter the other day from Ireland: the noble captain makes a handsome acknowledgement of his fault, and thanks me for my advice, which he tells me he shall follow; and I hope he will, but considering his way of life, his age, and hereditary constitution, it perhaps may be a task of too great difficulty to go through with: but he promises fairly, and that's all that can be expected from him, performance is another point.

Hendred October the 5th 1754

Dear Sir,

I think you was much in the right to make use of the fine open season we have had for all the out doors work; we too have something of that sort to be done, for the roof of our house lets in the wet in several places, upon very hard rains; but our bricklayer has been so much engaged in building of houses, that I have not been able to get him yet to repair mine; but he promises to be with me very shortly. I fancy the Axyard scheme must be laid aside at last; for upon my talking with Lady Cousin yesterday about her house, I find that she don't intend to let it ready furnished, the furniture being already disposed of; this I know is a material circumstance; for its being already furnished was a great inducement to my mother to take it, as she did not think it safe to bring what goods she had down into the country: another objection seems to lay against this scheme, and that is the rent, which her Ladyship sets at £20 per annum: these altogether are great rubs in the way; for here is a house at a large rent, considering the premises; to be either new furnished entirely, or else to be filled with unwholesome furniture from London; the expense of doing either of them being not small; these are considerations, which when duly weighed and debated at the next meeting of the House, will I fancy be a means of laying the scheme aside: I have by this post sent up my report to the Committee, and shall soon expect the result of their consultations upon it: what you say with regard to the obscurity of the place, is true enough; it is but an indifferent one for young ladies to shine in; nor can they indeed (as you go on to observe) shine in any advantage, till like the moon they are gilded and replenished with the cast off beams of a setting sun; and then perhaps, like what the poets feign of that same amorous orb, they'll meet with some Endymion or another, and take him to their arms.

I have been advised to drink centaury tea about an hour after dinner, which I have just now begun to do, and intend to continue it; for I have known it to be a great strengthener of the stomach, particularly in a sister of my wife's who has been vastly recovered by it; but this must be continued for sometime, before any benefit will be perceived by it: so this is a regimen, that I intend to pursue.

Hendred Nov. 9th 1754

Dear Sir,

I come no to the election at Sarum: in my last I told you what I thought of that matter; since which I had a letter from my brother Strother, who told me, that the Bishop did not stir in the affair at all, he supposed he had his reasons; but that one Mr. Hilman, (who is the Dean of Salisbury's son in law, and had been disappointed the last election, when the Bishop's brother was made a Canon) pushed on very hard, and had secured all the votes but one, and it was thought he would be the man; since this, on Thursday last I had a letter from the Bishop's Register at Salisbury, who tells me the election come on last Saturday, and Dr. Dodwell was chosen without opposition: this now is a circumstance, that staggers me much; because by the former account there must be a great opposition when the other gentleman is said to have secured every vote but one; so that how to reconcile these two contradictory accounts I know not: nor indeed can I pretend for the future to form any judgement, how the Bishop may be disposed to act with regard to me, or any of his more intimate friends and acquaintances: I think no one that I know, deserves greater tokens of favour from the Governors of our Church than Dr. Dodwell, his merits may demand the best preferments; and I am glad, though I have not the honour to be of his acquaintance, that he is thus distinguished; but at the same time, I have this concern upon my own account, that (if His Lordship has me at all in his thoughts) my turn is now at a greater distance, than I thought it was: though when I say this, I would not be thought to mean that I am uneasy about it, for I really am not; I shall still encourage the same hopes I had before, and only wait with Patience for his Lordship's pleasure and good will towards me: there's a very good prebend (that I believe won't be long before it's vacant) of £70 per annum the reserved rent, and a fine every seven years of £500, which I shall be well satisfied with, if his Lordship would give it to me: and there's another canon who is very old, and can't live long, so these may be very good openings for me or somebody else: but I have one favourite principle which is [? good to] stop the mouth of every complaint and silence all murmurings, upon such occasions as these; which is this, *whatever is, is right.*

I returned safe and sound from my expedition to the Devizes, which I mentioned in my last, and considering all things had a pleasant journey: I got a gentleman farmer of the parish to go along with me, who was acquainted with the road all the way, and a good travelling companion he was: my wife was in a peck of troubles about the gentleman collectors, for we had heard both from the public papers and several people, that they were very busy upon Marlborough Forest, and part of the road I was to go: but we had the good luck not to meet with them. The day we set out was very windy, and inclined to wet, which made it not so pleasant; we dined at Marlborough, which is twenty four miles from hence; we came here between eleven and twelve, and put up at the Famous Mount, which about four years ago was the dwelling place of the late Duke of Somerset; it is now let to an inn keeper, and I believe is the grandest inn in Europe: there are three ways from the public road into a large court yard, through which you pass in your way from London to Bath, it being so contrived by the present landlord, in order to draw the company to his house; and indeed by this and some other contrivances, he has got almost all the custom to himself, for you may now come to his house without going through the town, which is but ill paved and pretty steep in one part of it: this has drawn upon him the curses of all the other inns; but he seems to be a jolly good landlord, and not likely to lay this or any other thing else much to heart; the house is a noble large brick building, with two wings, sashed from top to bottom, at a distance from the hall door in the front of the house there is a large pavement of broad flag stones, here the coaches stop, from whence up to the door there is a handsome covered way in the Chinese taste, to secure the company from wet at their getting out and in of their coaches: the hall, at which you enter, is very much lessened by having the bar and the larder in it: the kitchen and offices are all under ground: the apartments are very handsome, but have been contracted by partitions, in order to make the more convenience for the present business of the house; but they are all very elegantly furnished in the best taste: the furniture was all new, and (I was told) cost above £3,000. There's a multitude of servants within and without, for the man has vast business: out of the hall you go down a flight of steps into the gardens, which are large, though not in that elegant order (you may imagine) as they were in the Duke's time; for now they are filled with useful things, and sheep are the only mowers of the bowling green: there is a greenhouse, large and sashed, but has nothing in it but hampers and lumber, there's a good canal, that empties itself into the Kennet, and has fish in [? it] it formerly was ornamented with rock work, but that is all gone to decay; the Kennet was close by the garden: through a handsome grove of trees, with a temple in the middle of it, you come to the foot of the mount, at the bottom of which, within an iron gate is a grotto; from the side of this grotto you begin your walk in a winding track of about ten feet broad, bounded by a quickset hedge, up the mount; it is reckoned a mile to the top, but so easy that you hardly find you ascend, the top is a broad grass plot with an octagon building sashed in the middle of it, from whence you have a beautiful and extensive view of the country all round: the hill is supposed to be an old Roman work, when they were in possession of that part of the island: after looking about us sometime we came down and met the waiter who came to call us in to dinner, the air of this place and the downs we had rode over before sharpened our appetites, so after eating a hearty dinner, and my companion smoking a solitary pipe, we set out for the Devizes, which is fourteen miles by the stones, most of it over wild downs, and ten miles of it upon the Bath road; pretty windy all the way, but no walk. In the room where we dined at Marlborough there was a pretty device, which took my fancy much: over the chimney there was a wind dial; it was a large square board painted with a blue ground, upon which was described in golden characters a circle with the thirty two points of the wind, as it is in a sailor's compass; there was in the middle of it a large gold hand, like that of a great church clock, which by a mechanical communication with the weather cock on the top of the chimney, showed you exactly where the wind was, as you sat in the room; and as it was a very blustery day, it was whimsical enough to observe the flutter it was in, by shifting its position so suddenly and so quick from south to west, and the several points between. Our business at the Devizes was transacted soon after I came there; so the next morning, with my bills in the lining of my waistcoat at my shoulders, we set out about seven for Marlborough, where we breakfasted, and about eleven set out for home; about twelve miles from Marlborough, we baited[1] our horses, and got to Hendred about five in the evening, after a very pleasant ride over the downs; where I found my wife overjoyed to see me safe returned.

Dec. 7th 1754

Dear Sir,

Just as the noble Captain came to Axyard, I had a letter from there, which told me, that he had ordered his party to Wantage, and that as soon as heard they were got there, he intended to come down to Hendred: as the small pox is so much at Wantage, I could not well be satisfied with this news; because there would then be too great a communication between the towns, than I thought would be safe; therefore I wrote immediately to Town, and told them how the case stood, and at the same time advised him to order them to Reading, but the very next morning after my letter was gone, two of his men (who came to Wantage the evening before) came here to enquire for their Captain; they seemed not well pleased in being ordered to a place so infected, where they themselves were in danger, and at the same time not likely to get any men. Their Captain came down to them on Wednesday after, and after staying little more than a week there, he came over to us last Saturday, and returns again tomorrow: he looks very healthy and well, and quite recovered the fatigue of his Irish campaign; the first day he was here, there was something in his looks that showed me how well acquainted I had been with his affair at Cork, he seemed a little abashed, and something tender I thought, when the conversation touched the wounded part, as it happened once or twice to do though in a very slight manner; after what he had said to me upon it in his letter before; I thought it would be a little ungenerous to put him to an open blush, so I let it pass without saying anything more to him about it: he has had but little success yet a while, having got but two recruits, that were brought over from Reading here last Tueday; he is going to move his quarters very soon to Newbury, and Friday next I think he is to go up to Town, in order to

---

1  Bait: to give food or drink to a beast, especially when on a journey.

celebrate my mother's birthday: I understand by all hands that she is greatly recovered in her strength, that she is able to go up and down stairs very well; by a letter from her to my wife last week, I find they have killed a porker, and she was then going down into the kitchen to make black puddings; so that by all these accounts she must be greatly altered for the better. When I wrote to you last, I was in great pain with a swollen face and a tooth ache; but I could bear it no longer than the Tuesday following, so I sent for an operator and had him out; which eased me immediately, and ever since I have been pure and well. That affair of Salisbury in favour of Dr. Dodwell I since understand was extremely fortunate; he had applied to the Bishop of London for his interest, who told him he was sorry he happened to be engaged for one Mr. Anberry and had accordingly desired two of the canons to give their votes for him; but (says he) if they can't succeed for him, I'll engage them for you; Dodwell went to Salisbury immediately, and told his friend Gilbert (the Bishop's brother) this; Gilbert he was sure of; he then applied to the Canon Sager, who is a friend of the Bishop of Winchester's; upon talking with him, he promised him his vote: so when the election came on, the Dean and another Canon voted for the Dean's son in law (Hilman) Morse and Wishart for Anberry, and Gilbert and Sager for Dodwell; here they were all at a stand, two and two; Anberry's friends finding they could not succeed for him, both come over to Dodwell, upon which the Dean and the other gentleman did the same; and thus he carried it by every vote in the Chapter; which I think was a very lucky thing for him; for at first setting out there was no great prospect of his succeeding: I am apt to think, as you do, this will throw me somewhat behind, but if I come in for something at last, I shall be well satisfied. I am sorry to hear so poor an account of Sir John, so that there is no hopes of any heir I see from him: but this is often the case, when the genial faculties are put upon their exercise too early.

Decr. 24 1754

Dear Sir,

My brother Tom is come to us this Christmas, who is no enemy to minced pies, and such sort of entertainment, as to be met with at this season of the year: when he was here this time twelvemonth, I talked to him about receiving the Sacrament, which he never had done in all his life; and for that purpose gave him some books, which he tells me he has read over more than once, but he has not yet been at the Communion; the reason he gives is, because he was ashamed, having nobody to go with him who had ever been there; so he is to go up to the table tomorrow with my wife; and he tells me, that he shall now always go, I hope he will be as good as his word, and be the better for it: I find he has a little cottage to himself, that he pays forty five shillings a year for, where he makes his own bed and dresses his own victuals, and seems by his talk to live quite agreeable to his own taste;

so that he may be said to be as happy as any man in England. I heard from Axyard last Sunday, they seem to have no complaints among them; if they had, we should have heard of them; Jack is returned to Reading, how long he stays there I didn't hear; but as he has got but one recruit (the other since discharged) I reckon he'll soon move his quarters; I am told we are to see him for a day or two again, before he goes off from our parts: they have heard lately from my brother at Virginia, who seems to be well satisfied with his station; that's good news I think.

Jan. 21 1755

Dear Sir,

My brother Tom was here when your letter came, and desired his duty to you and my aunt, when I wrote to you; he left us yesterday morning; and after staying about a week at home, he is to go up to Town, my mother having given him an invitation to Axyard: he did not intend, when he first came, to make us so long a visit, but the Archdeacon invited him to his Festival, which was last Friday; he tells me he wants much to see our garden in its perfection, and therefore intends to make us another visit for a few days about midsummer; I cant say, that either his or the Captain's company is such as I should like for a long continuance, for they are a great restraint upon my wife and I, as we cannot amuse ourselves with reading, or talking upon such sort of subjects as we usually do when we are by ourselves, because these two gentlemen have no sort of taste for such pastimes: the Captain at present is at Reading, but comes to us every now and then, to save expenses, as we desired he would. He has got but three recruits yet, and they are sent over to Ireland, his Colonel tells him their regiment is almost complete; as soon as it is, I reckon they'll be ordered back again to Dublin: but the Captain has met with so little success, that he never intends to come a recruiting any more if he can help it; and indeed I think it no desireable employment, for it leads them into expense, which they can't very well bear unless they have great good luck; they are to list none under 5ft. 7½ inches, no Irishmen, nor Papists; they are allowed £5 for every man, that is received by the regiment, when he is sent over; and out of this £5 they are to pay them perhaps one or two guineas for enlisting money, send them over with three good shirts, and subsist them at the rate of sixpence a day till they get to the regiment; these are hard terms, and not much to be got by the bargain; so that if they don't pass muster when they come there, the recruiting officer is all this money out of pocket; a brother recruiter of Jack's had the other day four men returned upon his hands and three more ran away before they got to the regiment, so that he is supposed to be a matter of £20 out of pocket: it is really a sorry life in all its stations, and what I would never advise any one to enter into; but he must now go through with it, be the consequence what it will.

March 1755

Dear Sir,

I reckon my mother has informed you, how my time was spent after I returned from Ditton; and that nothing material passed between the Bishop and me; as to the Duke, he was not at home. I set out on Saturday by five o'clock in the morning in the Abingdon machine, the day turned out very windy and wet; and as the roads were very bad, we did not get into Abingdon till past seven at night, where I found Joe with the horses, and a letter from my wife to desire I would not come home that night, if it was dark and wet; and as it really was so, I took her advice and lay at a friend's house in Abingdon, and set out early the next morning, though I had but a bad journey for it blowed and rained almost all the way full in my face; but I caught no cold: when I came home, I found my friend Seward there, whom I had so long expected, he came in the day before; he eased me in my duty at church that morning, by giving me a sermon, and on Tuesday morning after he left me, and set forwards for London: the next day I set out for Salisbury, having received a letter from Mr. Gilbert, who desired to see me as soon as I came to Town; I went to Penton that evening, where I stayed still Friday morning; between twelve and one I waited upon Mr. Gilbert who received me in the most friendly manner imaginable; insisted upon my taking up my residence in his house, where both his and Mrs. Gilbert's treatment of me was such, that I could not help examining my self, whether I was not a person of more distinction than ordinary, or whether I had not done them some signal service or other, which they were endeavouring to return by all this uncommon behaviour; but I could find no foundation for it in my self, and must therefore place it to the account of their own natural disposition to be agreeable to every body; Dr. Dodwell was then in residence; and upon my mentioning to Mr. Gilbert the Doctor's good luck in getting the canonry, and that it was owing chiefly to his friendly services, he said that he should be very glad to do me the same piece of service, which (you may be sure) I replied to in the best manner I could; I find that the Bishop is able to bring in who he pleases, and that the majority of the Chapter will vote for none, but those who have his recommendation; so that as I have reason to think, from their behaviour to me as well as from His Lordship's regards, that I am not an indifferent person to his Lordship I can't but flatter my self with some hopes of being brought in there some time or other; and as I know his Lordship's disposition very well, I shall not mention it to him; but let him serve me in his own way, for that I know pleases him best: I am now pretty sure, that the Bishop intended I should receive my fine before I exchanged my last prebend, because Mr. Gilbert said, that he could have told me five months ago, that I was to have this prebend; and perhaps (as he could have told me this) he might, if he thought it not improper, tell me of something else that may be intended for me hereafter: but as these things are not to be mentioned, it was a subject not fit for me to touch upon: soon after I came in he told me, that Dr. Dodwell and his Lady were to dine with us the next day, and I was to dine with them on the Sunday, and on Monday he and I would take a ride to the estate of the Bishop's a few miles from Salisbury, where his Lordship has a very pretty house; but I was obliged to excuse my self waiting upon them, as I was under a necessity of returning to Penton on Monday, my brother having engaged some company to dine with me there on Tuesday; and the weather being so uncertain, I was afraid I should not get back against Good Friday; so after some little altercation I was excused. Mrs. Gilbert has made me promise to bring my wife to Salisbury, which I shall take an opportunity to do the next time I go there; but that I fancy will hardly be till the summer after this, that is coming; for I have now preached my turn for the year 1755, and made an exchange for the tenth Sunday after Trinity 1756. I can't help thinking, by this extraordinary civility to me, that Mr. Gilbert is more apprised of my future fortunes, than I am my self; else why should he take notice of me, above all other common prebendaries? Why is my wife, above others, invited to Salisbury? What occasion is there for telling me in particular, that Canon Pile is old and can't endure long; and that Dr. Moss is ill at Bath? These are particulars, that can affect none, but those who are known to have expectations; or such as may be thought to listen with pleasure to hints of this sort, when the relater of them may be supposed to be in the secret: be it as it will, I think my prospect no bad one: I shall be glad to hear what your opinion is of this Salisbury tale. I set out from thence on Monday last, and stayed at Penton till Wednesday, when I got safe home in the evening about five, and found my wife and little ones pure and well; which is a full recompense for the fatigues of any journey at all; but I think this hurrying about has been of great service to me in point of health, as well as in other respects; for which reason I should not be uneasy at another call of the same nature.


July 12 1755

Dear Sir,

We were very glad to hear, by a letter from Axyard, that you and my aunt were very well on Monday last when the family were all at Ditton; I don't know whether they went to celebrate your wedding day or no; but if they did, my wife and I are in the wrong, for we drank both your healths upon that occasion the day after, which we have always took to be the proper day since the alteration of the style: however, be that as it will, you always have our sincere wishes for health and happiness, without any regard to days or style. I believe I have no occasion to give you a detail of the damages we lately sustained in our garden, from some malicious ill disposed people of the parish, for I imagine you have had that melancholy tale from my mother or my sisters, with all its aggravating circumstances; it was a spiteful thing (to say the truth) but who the delinquents were I know not; I published my manifesto upon the church doors, wherein I remonstrated the matter a

Constable's picture of Salisbury Cathedral and Close. Woodward often stayed there to perform his duties as prebendary. He never achieved his ambition of a canonry

*(Victoria & Albert Museum, London)*

little, by showing my concern at such ill usage from a parish, wherein I had always behaved as a friend to them all, and never wilfully gave any occasion for such treatment; at the same [time] assuring them, that I heartily forgave them this time; but if ever I should find any one guilty of the same another time, they were not to expect such indulgence, for it was transportation if not felony by the Black Act: I hope this will be theirs and my security for the future. I believe I mentioned in my last, that my wife and I were invited to Oxford the second of this month, where we accordingly went; we dined at Mr. Campion's chambers, a relation of my wife's; and when dinner was over, we went to the theatre, where my wife was greatly edified by a Latin speech, which was intended to be in praise of the several benefactors of the University; but the orator chose to depart from his subject, in order to introduce an invective against those, who are supposed to be enemies to our alma mater, and he laid it on very thick; but though my wife and the rest of the female audience were at a loss to know what he said, yet their attention was wholly fixed upon the violent agitations of the orator's body, which, as the subject required, was thrown into several whimsical postures, there being not a limb about him, nor a muscle in his face, but what was animated with a great deal of eloquence; and at proper periods he received the applause, which he seemed to wait for, by violent clappings from all his friends and acquaintance: he gave his audience to understand, that he himself too had his enemies, as well as his alma mater, who had spoken several reproachful things against him; but these enemies, whoever they were, had much better have let him alone, for he clawed them off most violently for it. There was a great deal of company there; and my wife had the pleasure to see the procession. When this business was over, we returned to Mr. Campion's and drank tea; after that we went to the music room, where we were entertained indeed with a fine assembly of gentlemen and ladies, and the oratorio of Judas Maccabeus most excellently well performed; this held us until nine o'clock, and then we went and supped with Mr. Campion's tutor; the next morning we breakfasted at Mr. Campion's, and dined with one Dr. Kelly a physician, a friend of ours, and about six set out for Hendred, where we got safe about nine, and found the two little ones well and fast asleep. As my disorder in my stomach had troubled me pretty much of late, I got Dr. Kelly to give me his advice, which he says will put me to rights; and if not, he tells me three weeks or a month at Bath will do it effectually; but I hope I shall have no occasion for such an expensive journey, for I think myself much better already, though I have but just begun my regimen; on Sunday evening last I took a vomit, on Tuesday a rhubarb potion with larden [? laudanum] ginger and other warm drugs; yesterday I repeated it, and am to ride out constantly every day, and take a preparation of the bark twice a day in pyrmont [? peppermint] water; this he thinks will effect a cure, so that I intend to follow his advice punctually.

Hendred Aug. 16 1755

Dear Sir,

We have lately had a visit from my brother Tom, who had promised to take a view of our garden in its summer dress; he came in to us on Saturday night about ten o'clock, having walked to Reading, which is twenty miles, and from thence he was conveyed hither in a higler's conveniency: my wife and I were at supper upon a small lobster; and it being Saturday night, the pantry was quite cleared of meat; cheese we had and apple tarts there were in the house, but he never deals in either of these; so what to do with a man so carnally inclined, who is none of your fancy eaters neither, we could not tell; I told him, I hoped he had supped; no says he I haven't, and I am confounded hungry; then (says I) you are come to the wrong house, at least you are come at the wrong end of the week, for we have not a bit of meat that's dressed in the house; well says he, if thats the case I'll do as well as I can; so we gave him a share of the lobster, which with a proper quantity of strong beer, sent him to bed with a light easy supper upon his stomach. I asked him once, how he managed about suppers, as he never eat cheese or apple pie; he said if he did not happen to be where there was meat, he often eat no supper at all, but smoked his pipe instead of it: whilst he was with us, we were to have some company to dine with us, the Warden of All Souls and his Lady, and another Lady and a Doctor of Divinity; I was somewhat at a loss how to dispose of him upon this occasion, for I thought such sort of company would be no entertainment to him; and (to speak the truth) I did not much care to show them such an uncouth relation of mine; so upon my mentioning their coming before him, he presently cried out he would steer another course as he termed it, for he never liked such fine folks; I pretended to expostulate a little with him upon it; but at last told him, that if he was so determined, he might meet with good entertainment perhaps at Abingdon fair, which happened on that day; and that he might not want employment, he should buy us some cheese there, which Jo was to do, had not this company come; he was well pleased with this; but unfortunately it proved a very wet day, and our company sent over in the morning to be excused, and they would come the next day; then we were again embarrassed, for there was no Abingdon fair the next day; however he himself thought of an expedient to disengage himself from the company he so much dreaded; so he very fairly invited himself to dinner with a young farmer and his mother just by; there he dined, and smoked his pipe, and spent his evening very agreeably (he said) at another person's house, where he also invited himself: so he quite got clear of the two Doctors and the Ladies. I had a letter last night from sister Charlotte, who tells me, that she never spent ten days so agreeably in all her life; as she did at Ditton, and expressed great obligations to my aunt and you for the civilities she received. Charlotte is a very good natured well disposed girl, and has a great many good, domestic qualities; a retired, rather than parading life, is more suitable to her inclinations.

Hendred Sep. 9th 1755

Dear Sir,

The day we were at Mr. Wymondesold's, a gentleman and his lady came in, at dinner time, from Wansted in Essex, who are to spend some time with them; they are very rich people I understand, and keep their coach and four; but little did I think, that they should know any thing of me: we spent the day very agreeably, for they are a couple of as fat, merry, laughing people, as ever I met with; after supper we were singing of songs, and upon my singing some particular song, the Lady said that Mr. George Woodward had sang it to her twenty five years ago; this surprised me much; but upon entering into the matter more particularly, I find she was acquainted with our family, whilst they lived at Westerham, being then a little miss upon a visit at a gentleman's house in that neighbourhood; and it seems I used to sing to her and call her my little wife; so we had a great deal of joking and laughing, upon such a discovery as this in the presence of my second wife: I think it was pretty extraordinary, that the Lady should remember me at such a distance of time, for I should have had no idea at all of her, unless she had roused my memory by some particular circumstances, and then I was able to tell her what her maiden name was. The week before last my wife and I went to visit a friend, about three miles on the other side Reading, at a place called Sonning; the house has the prettiest situation imagineable, it stands upon the brow of a hill, that overlooks the river Thames, which runs at the bottom of the garden, with the prospect of a fine country all about, adorned with woods and gentlemen's seats, and a view of the West Country barges passing before you, and shooting a lock, at the end of the grounds; the day after we came, we went after breakfast to Reading, and paid a visit to a daughter of my sister Strother's, who is at school there; at the same time we went to see a very ingenious piece of clockwork, which is a representation, by moving figures, of the several branches in the woolen manufacture, from the shearing of the sheep to the pressing and making of the cloth for sale; I think I never saw any thing, that came up to it, for there are a great number of figures, in various attitudes, and all at work at the same time; so that you see the shearer, the carder, the scribbler, the spinner, the weaver, the dyer, the hot presser, and several other artificers, at their proper employments, with every proper movement of their heads, hands and legs, that is required to carry on their business: the person who shows it, is the inventor himself, it has been the work of above twenty years, and well worth any one's seeing, for the price is but sixpence a piece. We stayed at our friends till Thursday morning, and after breakfast we set out, intending to stroll along at our leisure; in our way we stopped at Lord Fane's, about twelve miles from home, to see a very extraordinary grotto, all composed of shells and stones; and a greater variety, and so curiously disposed I never saw, far beyond Mr. Pope's or any else in England; the compartments are elegantly disposed, and several sorts of fruits and flowers are most naturally formed, with a vast deal of art and taste. There's a very pretty, little house, where the grotto is; about a mile and a half from my Lord's, which used to be a retirement for his Lordship's mother, who amused herself in making this grotto; it stands upon a pleasant spot with woods about it, and a pretty garden running down to the river, with hanging woods upon the opposite shore: when we had seen all that was to be seen, we went to a house just by, where we had put up our chaise, and here we got some coffee and bread and butter; and as we had ordered a cold roast of lamb to be ready against we came home, we had prepared ourselves well for it by a journey of twelve miles; for I thought we should never have done eating.

Hendred Octr. 4th 1755

Dear Sir,

The noble Captain, since his return to London from Colchester, seems to engross the regards of the whole family in Axyard so much, that they have had no leisure to acquaint us at all about them; and it is only from the latter, that we understand my mother is come back again: I wish your Chertsey scheme might be brought to bear, but I fear it will not, by what you say of that Lady's desire to live with them, who I think loves London best; and if that was not the case, I much question whether it would take effect; because I have observed, that there are people in the world who think that talking of these things gives them an air of consequence; they are prodigiously in love with retirement, and fond of the country to the last degree, should be vastly pleased if they could find out a pretty convenient box, with a garden to it, and a little parcel of land just enough for a couple of horses, because there would be no stirring abroad to church without some vehicle or other; but when some good friend has luckily found out a retirement of this sort, then some unforeseen objection or other crosses this delightful scheme, and puts a stop to it at once. The country is very agreeable to those, who are acquainted and used to the amusements, that are peculiar to it; but it affords very little delight to those foreign inhabitants, who meet not with the same customs of the place from whence they came: carts and road wagons do but ill supply the places of post chaises and coaches and six, nor is it all agreeable to an eye, that has been accustomed to politer objects, to be obtruded upon by a scraping country squire in boots and spurs. And without all dispute a country evening is but a melancholy point of time, when not employed in such parties and diversions, as receive their sanction from the taste and practice of the better sort of people: no wonder therefore, when a country retirement is thus circumstanced, that it should not generally meet with approbation from people of position. I fancy, if I was with you instead of Mr. Croft, your table would be but ill supplied with game, if you had any dependence upon my abilities in field sports, for I am not very dextrous at it, and at the same time a little too lazy; but though I am no sportsman, we have had a good share of game in our house, which has been sent in by our neighbours, because they know I can have none upon any other terms, than my obligation to their civilities. I am glad to find your oranges and myrtles are likely to revive again; indeed they looked to be in a very consumptive state, when I saw them, but I hope by proper care this next winter you'll perfectly recover them: as to our myrtles, we can get none to live with us; our oranges go on pretty well, they suffered a little in the cold weather; but by putting them into the hotbed they have got themselves into a tolerable good condition. This has been but a bad year with us for fruit; as to apples, I don't think we have two bushels in all. Our crops of corn hereabouts have been good, but a sad season to get it in; the harvest is not over yet. Great plenty of hares and partridges, and guns and dogs in proportion; foxes too I reckon we shall have more than usual, for we have a young fox hunting parson of good fortune, who is just married, and hired a house in our neighbourhood; he and a brother in law of the same stamp are to live together, and I suppose will stock the country with this sort of game; they will be no good neighbours for us, because I can't drink much strong beer, never go a hunting and don't much admire leather breaches; we have not seen them yet, but we intend next week to make the bridal visit, which will be continued with the same sort of ceremony that it begins with: the Archdeacon and I were very much pleased when we first heard of a clergyman's coming to settle so near us, (for the house is in his parish;) but as soon as we heard of the hounds, and the large quantity of strong beer that was laid into the cellars, it struck a great damp upon all our pleasing expectations; for we soon found we could be no good neighbours for him and his company, being entire strangers to the rules and doctrines of the chase: he is a young man just turned twenty four, and his Lady a virgin some few degrees on the other side of forty, who upon several accounts may not have good reason to expect much of her husband's company, and therefore in all probability will amuse herself in her solitary chamber, by tracing out with her needle the different fortunes of the chase, (which he is so strongly pursuing in the field) to adorn the parlour by way of fire screen.


Hendred October 25 1755

Dear Sir,

Your last letter was a very agreeable favour to us, as it was a full packet, and wrote with life and humour; which is a proof that you are in such health and spirits, as we always wish you to enjoy. The account you sent us, as you had it from Axyard, of my brother Harry's business to Williamsburg, was confirmed to us by the same post; where we were informed, that he has actually got a Captain's commission, and had sent to his mother for tent equipage; so I think he has had very good fortune at his first setting out; I could wish it was upon a better foundation; for in all probability, when the war is over, his Honour's income will be greatly lessened; and I am afraid he will not have the art to provide against such a change of his circumstances; for I think there are no half pay officers upon that establishment:

Jack too I find, both by letters and the public papers, has got a step higher, being promoted to a first lieutenancy: all this is matter of great joy and comfort to my mother, and I hope they may be lasting. Dr. Hume's[1] promotion, which you take notice of, is what we have been acquainted with for some time, but as this was a piece of secret history, we kept ourselves close, and listened to the stories of others who were more publicly talked of: Dr. Hume is a very ingenious man, and one who loves to do good, therefore I hope his promotion will be beneficial to his sister's family; and it must be great comfort to the Archdeacon, now in the decline of life, to see so near a relation advanced to such a station, who has no family of his own to share his favours: as I am not an utter stranger to Dr. Hume, am so intimate in his family, I shall think it worth my while to cultivate an interest with his Lordship that is to be, as it may be of service perhaps, sometime or other to little George, when he comes to the university: so you see how ready we all be to make an acquaintance with a rising man, in hopes of a lift ourselves: I have not seen the Archdeacon and Mrs. Spry, since I received your letter; but the first time I do, I shall be sure to congratulate them in your name. Mr. Penyston's marriage I saw in the papers, but have heard nothing of it yet from Axyard; I see they were married by Dr. Astrey, who is a relation of his, and one that he has great dependence upon; so I suppose it is a match to his liking; the Doctor has already been very kind to him, as I have heard; for he has given him something very handsome now in his lifetime; and after his death, it is said that he will have a good estate in Bedfordshire. We are sorry to hear that Molly Shepherd behaves so ill; but I have often heard her mother and her brother both speak of her, as not the best tempered young body: as to her mother's wanting her away to some other place, I know nothing of it; but if she does, I think she makes use of a very improper method to get her discharge, if she consults her own interest: but be this as it will, I hope neither my aunt nor you will show her more favour than she deserves, upon our account; for she was recommended to your service, as we thought it would be of advantage to her; but if she don't know how to behave herself, when she is well, she must look to the con-sequence herself, for we have nothing to say in her favour: we are glad to hear that your new man is like to do so well; we hope the same by our new maid, who came in the room of our cook; who left us only for another place where she has more wages; this being a liberty that my wife had given her, whenever she could meet with one to her liking. Our summer neighbours are now going to their winter habitations, some of them are gone already; and as we now expect our roads to get worse and worse, we shall soon shut up our chaise till next summer; unless we should have occasion for it, to carry us (if it can) as far as Wallingford sometime this winter, in order to take the stage for London; where we propose making a visit, and likewise at Ditton before we return; for we think this will be better, than to have these two visits to make next summer, when we propose going into Kent and

1   John Hume : Bishop of Oxford 1758 – 1766.

Sussex: we are not yet fixed as to our time of coming, whether before or after Christmas; but as soon as we have determined with ourselves, I shall not fail to make you acquainted with it; and one thing which inclines us to make this visit in the winter is, that I shall have an opportunity of seeing all my friends in town, besides being able to have better nights' rest in Axyard at this time of the year, than one has in the warmer months; but this is not to be given for a reason at all places. I think we were never worse off for apples, than we are this year; I don't think we have three dozen in the whole garden; we must be obliged to buy some for the use of the family: the orchards in general have not hit so well hereabouts, as they have done some other years. We are glad to hear, that you like your ducks so well, and hope you'll have a good breed of them next year: our neighbour Mr. Wymondesold has made us a present of some more of the same sort, but of a different colour; we are to send for them on Monday, and Joe is to carry a sack and bring us home some of his apples, as we have none of our own; he is the best neighbour, if a very rich one, that I know any where; they are extremely civil and obliging to us upon all occasions; which is not the character of all rich neighbours; a coach and six and a one horse chair don't always stand so well together.


                                                          Hendred Novr. 15 1755
Dear Sir,

The poor Archdeacon, we think, breaks a good deal; he is not very young, and was never a man of a strong constitution; the disorder in his eyes is very bad at this time; and as it is in his blood it affects his whole body in one respect or other, so that he is always under some particular regimen or other: it is a great comfort to him, I believe, now in this decline of life, that his brother Hume is coming into such a station as may render his family the less sensible of their loss in him, whenever he goes off: but we think it strange, that nothing further is done. I think you have entered upon a great undertaking, by being tutor to a Frenchman; could you but make him master of your integrity as well as your native language, it would be of great service to both kingdoms; and I would freely give my vote, that the whole French ministry should come to your school, with his most Christian Majesty at the head of your scholars. How strong the party may be in favour of Cardinals, either in Axyard or its suburbs, I know not; but this I know, that my wife intends to confront them with her Capuchin, that order at present being most agreeable to her interests; in my opinion (who have no great judgement in dress) of all disguises that the Ladies have chosen of late years, that of the Cardinal is the most surpassing; all that can be said for them is, that those who wear them do plainly show, that they have no design upon our sex; if I had any particular views in keeping my daughter single, I would oblige her never to appear without her Cardinal: poor Becky! She acts unknowingly against her natural inclinations, in pure compliance to an unbecoming fashion. I was surprised when you told me you had never seen a review, considering where you are situated; but I am glad to find that you was so agreeably entertained with it, for I think it is one of the finest sights, that I would choose to be present at. We are glad to hear that M. Shepherd has thought better of her place and her behaviour; I hope she'll mend as she gets older: her mother is coming away from her place, not for any dislike on either side; but her master has given her notice that he don't intend to have any person any longer in that station in his family, as a housekeeper.

I was obliged to take this piece of paper, to continue my narrative of Mrs. Shepherd; but don't know how to fill up any more of it, unless it be to tell you that little George is lately commenced-Latin scholar, and seems to be greatly pleased with the superiority he has gained over all the family except one, none but the parson of the parish being able to decline a noun better than himself; I am in great hopes he'll not be a blockhead, he shall not if I can help it; his memory seems to be pretty good, for (though I had never set him such a task) he repeated above a page to me in his grammar the other day, which he remembered only by reading it often: for I make him read some every day, and now and then I set him a little to get by heart, so that by degrees I shall make him pretty well acquainted with his grammar, before I send him to school; and then he will not have those difficulties to struggle with, as other boys who come raw to such exercises; discouragements at first setting out are apt to produce bad consequences: but if he is made acquainted with school exercises before he goes there, he'll find the advantage of it immediately, and go forward with more cheerfulness: Binny makes but a slow progress yet awhile, she is young and has her humours peculiar to that time of life, so that we are not always in a mood for reading; but that will all come to rights in due time; and there is not so great a necessity in getting girls forward in their books as boys; for they will be most of their time at home, and have but one language to learn.

Hendred Dec. 13th 1755

Dear Sir,

I have here enclosed a letter, which I received from an acquaintance of mine, who is well known in the world as a great antiquarian: he is a great curiosity himself, being in person, conversation, and dress, many removes back from the present times; he appears to be a member of the community some ages before the Reformation, his discourse most commonly taking its rise from old cathedrals and abbeys, whose very ruins are hardly in being; and the Abbots and Bishops of that distant age seem, by his way of talking, to be some of his most intimate acquaintance, as he calls several of them very familiarly by their Christian names: he's a gentleman of about £800 per annum, was formerly in Parliament for the town of Buckingham, but has hurt his fortunes in search of antiquity; for (old as he is at present) he is always making a pilgrimage to some old shrine or other, and his antique chariot and equipage generally excite the curiosity and speculations of the inhabitants wherever he goes: if you are a stranger to this gentleman, this delineation may be proper to make you acquainted with him: he came to see me some time ago, and the letter I here send you was the performance of his promise at that time. There is a particular circumstance in it, which I must explain to you, with regard to a namesake of mine: he was once asking me, if I knew one of my name, who lived at Ealing in Dr. Margey's parish; I told him that gentleman was my father; he asked me again if I had a brother whose name was Charles, I said I had but he was dead; he then told me a story of him, how he came to the town where he lived in company with a woman whom he called his wife; he said he was heir to a great estate, but that some misunderstanding happened between him and his father, on account of his marriage, but hoped it would soon be made up again: he called himself by the name of Carter, and asked Mr. Willis leave to shoot in his manor, and in the neighbourhood; he told him, as he was a stranger, he could not give him leave without the consent of the neighbouring gentlemen, upon which the gentleman took huff, and would not stay to drink a glass of wine, though the bottle was upon the table; a day or two after he marched off and left his madam behind him; and as she was very big, it was thought proper by the parish to have her examined before a Justice; it then appeared that the gentleman's name was Woodward, and his father lived at Ealing; but before they could get rid of her, she fell to pieces with two children who were baptised and died; and then she departed: Mr. Willis told me, that sometime after he had all his character from Mr. Nicholas Harding, who told him of his being in Kingston jail, with several more particulars; and as this was set down in their parish register, he sent me the extract of it: I can't but say I was a little out of countenance at this story of so near a relation, though at the same time I knew that my own reputation was no ways affected, by such an alliance.

Jan. 10th 1756

Dear Sir,

You take notice of the canonry of Salisbury being vacant, and ask me what I think of it; why I think it would be a pretty good addition to what I have; but I am many degrees below such high pretensions, as there is an own brother, a brother in law, and another near relation, who are candidates for every thing of this sort: I should not be displeased, if I was to succeed to a good living, which is made vacant by this gentleman's death; 'tis one of the churches in Reading, of about £300 per annum, a very good brick house, and less duty than any of the other parishes; 'tis in the Lord Chancellor's gift, and I dare say disposed of already, as the late incumbent by a gradual decay, gave very fair play to all those who had a mind to succeed him.

I had a letter last week from my brother Jack, who was come to Town to see what sort of a Christmas they spent in Axyard; they seem to be greatly engaged, as appears by all their letters, but whether it be in matters of much importance is known only to themselves; I wish that our coming to Town may not increase the fever of the family, and put the whole mass into a higher fermentation than it is at present; for what with contrivances in lodging this Berkshire parson and his wife, what with company to see and be seen by them, with several commotions of this sort, I fancy the house will be in no small confusion; and my mother's head but baddish these topsy turvy doings. When we get to Ditton, we shall all get time to breathe a little: there is one comfort in this winter expedition, that I shall have no bedfellows, that will be less than my wife; for of all summer houses, I like my mother's the worst. I believe we had a barrel of the same Colchester oysters, as you had, for ours were exceeding fresh and good: I am glad the arrival of your barrel has superseded the enquiry I should otherwise have made, after Charlotte and her promises.

Feb. 7th 1756

Dear Sir,

I am very glad to find, that after having been embarked so long in a law suit, and suffered so much in that ruffling profession, you at last see land, and at so short a distance from you; as you have so good a pilot, and so fair a wind, I hope we shall hear you are safe landed, by that time we come to Ditton: our journey to Town is now fixed for the 13th of this month, we are not yet come to a determination, what day we shall pay our duties to you and my aunt; but with that we'll acquaint you time enough, when we get to Axyard: you seem to be afraid that our coming there will somewhat embarrass my mother's present family; we some time ago thought so too, and mentioned our apprehensions in a letter; but we are told that it will be no inconvenience at all, as we are to find when we come there: I suppose they have a bed in the neighbourhood at their service, otherwise I don't see they can dispose of us all. My sisters have a very careless way with them in their correspondence; they not only put one to some trouble in guessing at their words and expressions, but they likewise are very forgetful of the subject that one writes to them upon, and never send one a direct answer to any enquiry that we make, be it what it will: a negligence of this sort is greatly detrimental to themselves; because, instead of answering a letter that is wrote to them, (which would help them a little forward upon their blank paper), they are under a necessity of making a great many idle excuses for the shortness of their letters; which are generally little more than an enquiry after the health of us all at Hendred, that my mother's head is bad or she would have wrote herself, and that company is just come in else they would write a longer letter. These are some of those slips, which is owing to the whirligig of their natural constitution, and what I have more than once given them a friendly hint of, but I am afraid they are in corrigible, for I can never see any symptoms of amendment.

Feb. 7th. Being afraid that I should not have time on Saturday to write all my letter, I began it and got this far on Thursday; because we expect Mrs. Price from Lockinge here today, and then I knew I should only have the evening for this business: 'tis now about nine o'clock, and we look for her to breakfast, as the morning is pretty fair and good walking, in the mean time then I may go on with my letter. We had the fullest church here yesterday, that I ever saw, and I should have hoped it was owing to something better, than the common curiosity of hearing what is said upon such a new subject, had not I observed the congregation somewhat lessened at the evening service; 'tis a difficult matter to convince country people, or indeed others of a better education, that their main business at Church is to attend to the prayers rather than the sermon, which is the lowest part of the service — Mrs. Price is come in, and I must now leave off for breakfast — she is gone, candles are lighted now and I have taken up my pen again. You have often heard me speak of Dr. Cooper of this parish, as an odd sort of a man, conceited of his own abilities and very over-bearing in his talk: he has lately had a quarrel with a substantial young farmer of this town, at his own house, which began with words and ended in blows, the Doctor being a gentleman taking the privilege of giving the first blow; but the farmer gave him his just deserts by banging him very heartily, so that he did not go out of his room for above a week, and then went off to London and is not yet returned, however the Doctor is so generous as to own, that it was his own fault, as he struck the farmer first: I hope it will make him a little more orderly for the future, for he is apt to take to great liberties with his tongue.


                                                      Hendred May 29 1756
Dear Sir,

Jack I understand is going for Dover, and how he is to be disposed of afterwards I don't hear: my mother they say is but very low spirited, on account of her two sons, whose present condition in life is I think by no means agreeable, but it was their own choice, therefore they must make the best of it. The Bishop of Salisbury held his Visitation at Abingdon this day sennight, and gave us an admirable good charge, with regard to the behaviour of the clergy in general; his Lordship was very cheerful, and I had the pleasure of spending an hour or two with him after dinner, with a few select friends, before he set out for the Bishop of Oxford's, where he was going upon a visit.

When I wrote to you last, I talked upon the subject of recruits; but little thought that we had one raising in our own house at that time; since that we have made a discovering of this sort; it was our under maid, who came to us last Christmas, and a very good servant she was, we all liked her much, as being an active, diligent and neat girl; and one that we thought was better disposed than ordinary: however, my wife suspected something and upon taxing her home she owned it, upon which she was immediately discharged and advised to get herself married, as soon as she could: the banns were accordingly put up last Sunday for the first time; the young man had been her fellow servant about three years ago, and had kept her company ever since; they intended to be married next Michaelmas, but unfortunately could not stay quite so long. We have now got quite a young lass indeed; she's a niece of our maid Sarah's, and a very sober girl, well grown for her age, and of very sober honest parents, who live in the parish; her aunt has undertaken to instruct her, and give her the best assistance she can, who is an excellent good housewife herself; therefore we are in great hopes she'll improve well under such a tutoress. I dare say your garden looks very beautiful at this season of the year, especially as your flowers are always disposed with the exactest judgement, and the most elegant taste; the weather of late has been very prejudicial to the wall fruit, though for our parts we have none to be hurt; but it is a general complaint all round us. If I was to see Mr. Croft, I believe I should second your motion for a post-chariot, it being a far more convenient machine for them, than what they have.

The Archdeacon has received great benefit by the Bath, and looks better than he has done for many years; he and Mrs. Spry desired their compliments to you and my aunt, when I wrote next. I hope you'll have a pleasant jaunt to the great town, whenever you go, and that my aunt is returned safe and sound to Ditton, and left all friends well.

Hendred June 25 1756

Dear Sir,

I hope the warm weather, that is now come in, has carried off your cold, and that you have been able to pay your intended visit, though nothing was said of it in a letter that we had from Axyard by Wednesday's post. I reckon you have had as great rains with you, as we have had here; they have done a great deal of good, both in the fields and the garden: our farmers rejoice in the prospect of a plentiful crop of all sorts of grain; and we are in hopes of a great many apples, which is the only fruit, that is likely to come to good with us; and that is a useful fruit. You seem to think of your London visit being returned the seventh of next month; we shall remember you upon that day, though not at home; for we shall then be at Oxford, being invited to the Commemoration, when particular honours are to be paid to Lady Pomfret, who has presented the University with a fine collection of ancient statues, and such like curiosities; there are to be oratorios, speeches and verses spoken by the young noblemen and gentlemen commoners; my muse among others will make her appearance there, in the person of a Scotch Lord: for the Archdeacon's son who has no genius for such performances, and being obliged to provide verses for his pupil, who is Lord Glenorchy, has requested a copy from me, which I sent him last week: I am under a sort of obligation to Mr. Spry, for some pictures of his own drawing which he gave me sometime ago; and he is now drawing two more for me, which are to hang on each side the Duke of Grafton in the best parlour: they are in Indian ink, and very well executed; he has a great genius in this art; and the painter and the poet you know have always been great cronies.

There has been another vacant canonry at Salisbury; as soon as I heard of it, I wrote to Mr. Gilbert, and requested the favour of his vote and interest, if he was not already engaged; but that very night I saw it in the papers, and that it was to be filled up by the Bishop's nephew: soon after I had a very handsome letter from Mr. Gilbert, who says that this canonry is not elective, but absolutely in the Bishop's own gift; that he was in Town when his Lordship heard of it, and that the Bishop had then made a tender of it to the person he designed it for; which I suppose is Mr. Sherrard, Mrs. Gilbert's nephew, though Mr. Gilbert mentions no name: he tells me, this is not known to any body but himself, therefore it will not be proper to talk of it any where else; but I thought I might acquaint you with it. There is another old Canon, whose death has been expected a long while, who will succeed him I can't say, but as the Bishop has now provided well for all his new relations, he perhaps may think of his friends for the next vacancies: I don't intend to make any more applications, let what will happen, for Mr. Gilbert knows my intentions; and it will be in his power to serve me more than any one else, if his Lordship intends me any further favours.


                                                                July 10th 1756

Dear Sir,

You deserved to have a letter at our return from Oxford, which was yesterday in the evening; and I would not have lost the sight of such a celebrity (as the term in vogue is) for ever so much; for I believe there never was (at least for many years past) such a concourse of people of all ranks and distinctions; Oxford hardly ever before saw such a crowded theatre for three days together: as we were told the solemnity was to be opened by ten o'clock on Tuesday, we thought it best to be there overnight; and we were invited to Corpus Christi College, to meet the Campion family, who stopped there in their way to Warwickshire, where they are gone upon a visit to some relations, so we set out in the afternoon, and supped with them and some other friends at Corpus, the next morn we went to their lodgings, and about nine went to the Theatre; but such crowds were got to the doors, that it was with difficulty we got in, and had the good luck to get seats, where we had a full view of the procession, that was to be made by Lady Pomfret and her retinue: about eleven it began; the doors were thrown open, and in they came with the beadles before them, the music playing a most grand march with trumpets, French horns, and kettle drums; Lord Westmoreland led Lady Pomfret, Lord Litchfield and Lady Westmoreland, who were followed by several other Lords and

Ladies too many to be mentioned, the nobility and gentry all dressed in their doctor's gowns, as having had those honorary degrees conferred upon them sometime before; the Duke of Beaufort is so lame with the gout, that he took his seat sometime before, as not being able to join in the procession; after these came the Vice Chancellor and all the Doctors and Heads of Houses in their proper habits; they were all received with a continued clap of applause by the whole theatre: as soon as they were seated, the Vice Chancellor in a short speech acquainted the audience with the occasion of the solemnity, then the Poetry Professor made his speech; these two were in Latin: you must observe, whenever any speaker mounts the rostrum, the whole audience clap him, and so they do when he has done: after these five young noblemen, and a gentleman commoner recited verses in praise of Lady Pomfret's benefaction: Lord Litchfield, Lord Charles Spencer, Lord Willoughby de Broke, Lord Glenorchy, and Sir Wyndham Knatchbull Wyndham, and one Mr. James, a young gentleman of Barbados bred at Eton school. They all spoke very handsomely; but none like Mr. James, who in several parts of his recital received the applause of the theatre; for he was a genteel person, good voice, and a fine action; he had been under the direction of Dr. King for some time before, who is the most complete orator of the age. These were the speakers for the first day. As soon as they had done, we had the Coronation anthem, and then her Ladyship etc. went out in the same triumphant manner she came, the music playing a march, and the whole theatre paying their respect to her and the rest of the nobility and gentry with loud claps, as they passed along: there could not possibly be anything more grand and solemn, every one showing the greatest delight imagineable at the appearance. We then adjourned to dress ourselves for dinner; we dined at Corpus with the Campion party, and at three went again to the theatre, for we were obliged to go soon, or else we should have had no places; here we met with the same noble company again, and heard the oratorio of Judas Maccabeus; it was over about eight; we then went to Maudlin Walks, to see the company, and returned to Corpus to supper. The next day was the same as the first, only different speakers, and a different oratorio (which was Joshua). The speeches began with that of the University Orator, who was succeeded by five gentlemen commoners, one of which was Mr. Barrington (brother to Lord Bolingbroke) who spoke an extreme good one in praise of the liberal arts; this was in prose, and all his own, and delivered with the finest grace imagineable, both of voice and action; every one was charmed with him; he was an Eton scholar; and so was Mr. Knight (son of Broadnox May Knight), who only wanted a clearer voice to excel every one, who went before him; for there was the greatest propriety of action, and the finest and most becoming address, that one could wish to see; had the fathers and mothers of these young gentlemen been there, they could not have contained themselves, they must have burst with joy and ecstasy; I own for my own part, their behaviour brought tears from my eyes more than once; and so it did from others also; for the whole audience in general seemed to be in raptures at the sight, and gave the utmost testimony of universal approbation. All the speeches were in verse, (except Mr. Barrington's) some Latin and some English: but my verses were not spoke, the Dean of Christchurch having given orders, that none of that college should speak any thing, but what was made in Christchurch, so his Lordship was obliged to repeat a Latin copy, which without vanity I may say was not so good as those he had from Hendred. The Eton gentlemen were the crack of those two days, who did honour to my old school and to the university too: as I had been a member of both, it gave me infinite joy: these young speakers are now all distinguished by silver tufts upon their caps. When this was over, there was an occasional anthem, and then they marched out as they did before: we then went to dinner again at Corpus, and supped there in the evening; for the gentleman, who entertained us, was Mr. Campion's tutor, and had been with him a week at our house last spring twelve month, so our eating and drinking cost us nothing at our inn where we lay, nor did we pay for our beds, as our horses were there; for lodgings were most monstrous dear at private houses, and at inns too, if people had no horses with them. On Thursday morning we went to the Campions and took our leaves of them, as they then set forward on their journey; after this we went to the theatre, which was filled in the same manner as it was the two preceeding mornings: but there was no more speeches now, the only business was conferring degrees upon several gentlemen in honour of Lady Pomfret. It was a difficult part that her Ladyship had to act; to behave in such a manner, as to show she was not insensible of the honours that were performed to her, and yet not vain of the praises she was bound to hear: her behaviour was proper, and very becoming; who seemed to be more pleased with the opportunity of having the University appear to so great advantage, in the eyes of every one that was there, than she was with the encomiums that were made upon her own self. This morning solemnity concluded with the Coronation anthem; we then dressed ourselves for Christchurch, where we were engaged to dine with Mr. Spry; the Archdeacon and Mrs. Spry (who came from London the evening before) dined with us, and some other company; after dinner we went to the Theatre again, and heard the music; this was the conclusion of the whole celebrity: the evening we spent at Mr. Hume's (a brother of Mrs. Spry's, who is an apothecary in Oxford). Yesterday morning we breakfasted at Mr. Spry's at Christchurch with his father and mother and one of his sisters; then we walked about, and see the company that was setting off for their own homes again; for the streets were full of coaches and six and post chaises etc. All the forenoon, ladies and gentlemen of all ranks moving about from one place to another: about noon we ordered a scrap for our dinner, and then set out for Hendred, where we arrived safe and well, and found all well there; only the family somewhat increased: a duck that had been missing for sometime was brought home with a brood of twelve young ones, very stout and strong: a hen had presented us with nine young chickens, and a cat was brought to bed with five or six unhappy little things, that are all born to be drowned.

Brenchley August 1756

Dear Sir,

We were in so great a *flutteration* when we had the pleasure of meeting you and my aunt at Kingston, that we had scarce time to make you both a proper acknowledgement for the favour of your company, though it was but for a very short time; we were extremely glad to see you, and took it very kind of you, that you would give your selves the trouble to look upon three dirty travellers; we hope you got safe home. I reckon you went on in fear and trembling, till you got into the lane. As to ourselves, we had a good pleasant journey to Croydon, where we dined, and as the inn was repairing, and workmen about all parts of it, we took up our station by three in a pretty summer house upon the bowling green, where we eat our morsel; about four o'clock we set forward, and had a most delightful country quite down to Sevenoaks, where we got in about nine o'clock, only stopping a few minutes at Farnborough to water our horses and ourselves: this was a long stretch, forty seven miles; the day before was forty one: we then had but eight or nine miles to Southborough, where we got the next morning by breakfast time: I don't find that either horses or men were at all the worse for the journey: the morning after we came there, we went down to Tunbridge Wells, which is two miles and a half, where we strolled about for a few hours, and then returned to dinner; George was highly delighted with all these new things, and came away sixpence poorer than you and my aunt sent him from Kingston, by happening to drop into a toy shop. I would have preached for the gentlemen at Tunbridge Wells last Sunday morning, but the pulpit happened to be engaged; so I went with my brother Latter to a church of his about eight or nine miles off, (which he supplies one part of the day) and gave him a sermon. We then returned home to dinner, and at four in the afternoon his other church begins, which is about a mile from his house, (for he lives in his own house, not in the parsonage) and there I preached for him again; so I was not very idle all the day. On Monday my brother and I went to Tunbridge Town, which is about five miles from the Wells, (his house being just between both) where there was a meeting of gentlemen who are proprietors in the river, that was made navigable there some few years ago; he is one of them: we had a very handsome dinner at the expense of the Trust; here the accounts were audited, and orders passed relating to the navigation: my wife and sister Latter came to the town in the afternoon to pay a visit to a sister of my brother's, who lives there, so we returned all together in the evening. The next day (which was Tuesday) was exceeding wet from morning till the evening; we happened to be engaged to dine at the gentleman's, who is Minister of the Wells, and was to go to the ball that evening; we should have been glad to have had a better day; but we brushed through and went to the ball; where was a great deal of company, but none of any great account, several being engaged in the public business, and others gone to visit the camps, which seems to be greatly in vogue at present: George went with us to the ball, and was greatly pleased, as he never had seen any thing like it before; his remarks were very odd and uncommon, and made us laugh heartily: about nine we came away, and as the moon was not up we got safe home by the light of a flambeau, that Joe carried in his hand as he rode along with us; it was a very calm evening and no rain. The next morning we set out for Brenchley where I am at present; we were very much affected by the roads after all this rain; but my brother Courthope sent a servant to meet us, who conducted us a good way through the grounds, so we found no inconvenience at all: it is about eight miles from Southborough; we got here about dinner time, and in the afternoon walked away about a mile to see a fine cricket match; they had not time to play it out that night, so they went to it again yesterday morning; we went to see it after breakfast, and a finer match was never seen; there was a great deal of variety and turns in the game; when the two last men went in, they wanted three to tie the Brenchley men, four would beat; they got three, and before they could get another, one of the gamesters knocked up his own wicket with his bat, which occasioned great shouts; so the game was won by neither side: we returned to dinner, and in the afternoon played at four handed cribbage, my brother and sister Latter being with us here for a few days — thus endeth my tattle.

Uckfield Sepr. 4th 1756

Dear Sir,

My last was dated from Brenchley just after we came there. We had formed a scheme of going to the Hanoverian camp[1] near Maidstone, but the ways and the weather prevented us, for it was but ten miles from Brenchley; so that I can give you no account of our diversions, there being none but what we made at home amongst ourselves, and the company of some of their neighbours: I went over to Ticehurst, where I spent two nights, and took George with me who rode before Joe, the roads being too bad for a chaise; so that as my wife could not go herself, I was willing to have something with me that was nearest to her in likeness; you may guess at the reception we met with from the whole parish, amongst whom I spent so much of my time just after I went into Orders, and who were so well acquainted with those early regards I have so long had for her, who is now my wife; the sight of our little boy pleased them much, many of whom knew his mother from her birth: this journey, I thought, made me look upon myself as a very old fellow, when I saw so many grown up men and women, whom I had christened, some of whom were married and had children; so that in my pastoral capacity I was really a grandfather. Whilst I was at Brenchley we had a visit from a lady who lives near the Wells; she told us that the Duke of Newcastle was there for about half an hour such a day; for a friend

1  Coxheath, the military exercise ground in Kent.

Ticehurst Church, Sussex, where Woodward spent eight years as a curate. It contains several memorials of his wife's family, the Courthopes

(*S.A. Davies*)

of hers called her out of her lodgings, on purpose to see his Grace walk up and down the Walks, without any one with him except his nephew Shelley: this sure must be a great mortification to him, to find that none of the company showed him any respect, who but a few months ago would have been pressed almost to death, by crowds of his admirers and humble suitors; after walking sometime in this manner he at last came up, and spoke to a gentleman that I know, who never was in his interest, and took two or three turns with him, every one else retiring at a distance and leaving the walks clear for him; he just went into the rooms and to the well, dispersed his gratuities to the book keepers and the dippers, and so went off for Sussex, though he told them he would be at the ball in the evening: the bad weather we lately had, has carried off a great deal of the company from the Wells; it has not been a very full season, and those who were there were none of the best fashion. The roads were so bad, and the wheels of our chaise so much too wide for the ruts, that we got my brother Courthop to send his post chaise over for us, to fetch us to Uckfield last Wednesday; so we came as far as the Wells in our own, where we met the chaise, and so came hither by dinner time; but a very bad way it is, even in a good summer: next Monday we go to Danny and return here again on Thursday; so I'll stop here till our return.

Uckfield Saturday morn:

We returned hither from Danny on Thursday by dinner time: the day we went thither, we met a great deal of fine company at dinner, Mr. Pelham's family of Stanmer who is one of the Knights of the Shire: the next day we were all invited to Stanmer, which is about seven miles from them; my brother Courthop had sent us in his post chaise to Danny[1], so we had the use of that whilst we stayed: here we met a great deal of other company, several of whom were my old acquaintance; and a most sumptuous entertainment we had, and served up in a grand manner; my wife I do assure you had that respect showed to her, as to be placed the second lady at the table, Mr. Spence's Lady (whom my aunt perhaps may have some knowledge of) was the only one above her; as to giving you any account of the dinner, I can no more pretend to it, than I could to describe the birthday clothes at Court: the house itself is a very neat pretty building, and very elegantly furnished, not so large indeed as some others that I have seen, but altogether a very pretty place: it stands upon the Downs, though in a bottom with a wood behind it, that is laid out prettily in a serpentine walk along the side of it, with flowering shrubs between the walk and the wood: the behaviour of the joint proprietors of this pretty spot is very engaging, both of them being esteemed by all for their courteous affability to all their company; and what sets their character in a higher point of light than usual, considering their rank, they have prayers constantly every night in their family; the clergyman of the parish, who lives just by them, dines with them every day and performs the office; and though he is frequently

2   Danny: possibly the place name in Hurstpierpoint, Sussex.

out of order with the gout, and not able to be there, yet Mr. Pelham don't catch at that excuse (as some perhaps would do) but he reads prayers himself: in short they are the best people I ever heard of, being respected by the rich and beloved by the poor, to whom they are very great friends; as I have learnt from several stories they tell of their goodness and condescension to this rank of people: we performed nothing more of any note, whilst we were at Danny, except this visit which has taken up so much of my paper; and on Thursday after breakfast we returned to Uckfield; 'tis about seventeen miles: presently as soon as we have breakfasted, we set out for my brother Latter's at Southborough.

We are glad to say that our duck and drake have not lost their genial faculties, by removing from Hendred to Ditton, you have had good luck with your young ones I think; the method we use in fattening of them is this; we confine them to some little place, and feed them with barley meal made into pudding, Molly Shepherd knows how I mean I fancy; 'tis only water and ground barley mixed together. You tell me that you'll send me some more franks, when I get to Axyard; you'll be pleased to send them there ready for me, because we shall stay but two nights in Town; we shall get there next Monday sennight, and go out on Town on Wednesday morning.

Monday Night Hendred
September 1756

Dear Sir,

I reckon you have heard by this time, that we did not set out from London till Friday morning; we lay at a friends at Sonning that night, which is three miles on the other side of Reading, and got safe home on Saturday to dinner; where we found our little girl in good health and spirits, and very glad to see us again. At our return from Uckfield to Southborough, where we spent our last week before we came to Axyard, we found nothing more by way of entertainment than what we had seen before; the company at the Wells was somewhat lessened; and declined apace whilst we were there; so that there were but few families left when we came away. My wife and I were under some concern, at the thoughts of taking up our lodging in Axyard, after we had slept so comfortably in Kent and Sussex; but to our great joy we were informed, soon after we came into the house, that the enemy had evacuated the place, and not one of them was to be found in all those parts: we could hardly give credit to such a piece of good news; but we were very glad the next morning, that we could so well certify the truth of it; for we slept very quietly, and had no manner of disturbance from bugs or any thing else; I find it has cost my mother above £6 to get rid of these troublesome tenants; and I verily think she never laid out such a sum to a better purpose; for a good night's rest is no small satisfaction to people of all conditions. Our stay in Town was so short, that I did not attempt any visits.

When I came home, I found the Critical Review of last month. I am told the chief person concerned in this work is Johnson the Dictionary man, a person noted for great invectives in all his writings, and much ill nature in his private character: the Monthly Review (they say) is a much better thing; I believe I shall change for that.

By our being absent so long, we have a good crop of grass in our field for our horses; and as to the garden, that is a perfect wilderness; it will help to carry off some of Joe's bad humours, that he may have contracted by his frequent regalings in Kent and Sussex, before he gets the better of the grass and weeds.

Hendred Octr 20 1756
Saturday morn.

Dear Sir,

I had a letter last night from my brother Jack, who I find is marched from Dover, and is got to Languard Fort, where he complains much of the badness of its situation, and ill accommodation, being not allowed either bedding, candles, or firing, as is usual in other garrisons; and as they have no town or village nearer than three miles, he is obliged to send as far as that for milk for his tea; if it was not for a butcher, who visits them twice a week, they should be quite starved: he tells me that he ranks as a Captain, and has 4–6 a day, and his Colonel says, that he has been so well represented to His Royal Highness the Duke, that he stands fair for the next vacant company, which I am very glad to hear of; for I believe Jack is very diligent in his profession, and deserves to be taken notice of; I find he has got leave of absence for two months, and is going up to Town. I want much to hear of poor Harry, who is but in an uncomfortable situation in America, if he is at all; for they have heard nothing of him for several months, as far as I can find; poor boy! I wish he had been behind a counter in Thames Street, selling of cheese, or anything but a soldier. I had almost forgot to tell you that my good friend the Duke of Grafton seems to make himself merry with these displacings at Court; for as he is not likely to be removed, he in a droll way gave an invitation to all his old friends, who were upon the move, that they might take a parting glass together; I can very well figure to my self, how His Grace behaved at the head of his resigning company upon such an occasion: I dare say he was full of his quaint speeches to them, and made them pure and merry.

December 1756

Dear Sir,

I don't find that this frosty weather, which we have had for some time past, has done us any harm within doors; slight colds we have all had, but nothing of any great consequence; cauliflowers and some other young things in the garden have been injured by it, but these may be repaired some time hence: our greatest complaint in these parts, is the dearness of bread corn, which is an article that affects all ranks of people in their several proportions; but the poor especially must be greatly distressed by it, eight shillings a bushel being more than they can afford for bread, out of six shillings a week; so that they are obliged to make use of other sorts of grain for their present subsistence: but it is to be hoped this extravagant price will not hold much longer.

Our great and good neighbour, Mr. Wymondesold, left the country yesterday morning; his parish will feel his absence, for he does a great deal of good amongst them, and employs a great many poor people: he has this and the last summer been about a very good piece of work; he has undertaken the repair and beautifying of his parish church, (the Living is in the gift of All Souls College, Oxford) and he has made it from a little, dark, indecent place, one of the prettiest, neatest churches that we have any where at all; the pews have all been new built in a more commodious manner, the reading desk, clerk's seat, and pulpit, all enlarged and new painted, the chancel well repaired, and the Commandments, Lord's Prayer, and Belief, new done, and properly placed, the monuments cleaned, windows new glazed, with large crown glass, the pavement all new, with two handsome new porches at the north and south doors; the doors new painted, and the whole church both inside and out rough cast and white washed: and he is now employing people about making the ways about the village better, opening a little stream that runs through it, and sloping the banks, and planting trees upon the sides of it in regular rows, which will make it a sweet pretty place; and before it was as unsightly a thing as one could look upon: these and several other such things are his constant amusements whilst he is down here, besides clothing poor people, and doing several acts of charity amongst his neighbours. A man of his disposition cannot but be of great use where he lives, and as he is a very courteous, sensible man, we think our selves happy in such a neighbour.

Jan. 15th 1757
Hendred.

Dear Sir,

It is now exactly a month since the date of my last letter; I had thoughts of writing again this day sennight, but was willing to stay another week.

I never hear any thing worth repeating from Axyard, whose letters are all filled with fiddle faddle stuff about great weddings, fine clothes and fashions; and now and then some remarkable transaction, which I have read in print the post before: Jack has been at home I hear for these six weeks, and we knew nothing of it, till last post, though we have frequently asked the question, as he had told me the beginning of November, that he should go to Town very shortly for two months; but it is their way never to answer one's letters; they write often it is true, but they never return an answer; and the reason is, they never look upon any letter they have received when they set down to write, so that we seldom have any return to any of our questions, be they what they will. Our Christmas entertainments are now almost over; we are to go to the Archdeacon's on Monday, it being their wedding day, and this will finish the minced pie season; my brother Tom is with us still, I reckon he intends to take his leave of us, as soon as he has tasted the minced pies at the other Hendred, for he has had his share of all that was eat at our Hendred; and very happy, I believe has has been ever since he has been with us, as his taste chiefly lies this way: though we have endeavoured to entertain him in another way, by setting before him some dishes of Mr. Fielding's cookery, in his History of Tom Jones. He is so pleased with the book, that he intends to purchase it: as to his behaviour here, it has been very well and decent; for I believe he has left his drunken companions, and lives a good sober life; I never observed him at all eager for liquor, and his smoking is very moderate; one pipe before breakfast, and perhaps one after supper, is all he takes; unless he is pressed to it by any one that is in company: he tells me, that he is much obliged to my mother for her care of his daughter, and shall not fail of contributing his four guineas a year towards her maintenance; and I hope he'll be as good as his word, for he's a very good natured poor fellow, and very honest.

Hendred
Feb. 5 1757

Dear Sir,

I am in hopes the frost is now going off, for it seems to be a thorough thaw at present: I have not kept myself entirely by the fireside all this hard weather, but have been out almost every day, purely for exercise; last Sunday indeed I took a walk after dinner of five miles, to supply a church for a friend who is absent, and did intend to come home that night, but the snow prevented me; so I lay there, and returned the next morning after breakfast, and extreme good walking it was; after resting about an hour I went to church, read prayers and preached; and after evening service we went to dinner; all which agreed with me very well. I hope now we shall have a little better weather, though I can't but say what we have had has been very seasonable, and I am in hopes we shall feel the good effects of it next harvest; the poor people have had a bad time of it, and as to corn and firing it is not much better still: we have set a collection on foot for their present relief, but I am afraid it will be of little service, as there are but few in our parish, who are able to contribute much; I gave them a guinea to begin with, and did intend to go round the town my self yesterday with the officers, but it was so very snowy, that I did not care to venture, so how it has turned out, I have not yet learned. I see by the papers, that several

East Hendred High Street as it is today

(S.A. Davies)

parishes have considered the distress of the poor, during the inclemency of the season, in a very handsome manner. You see Mr. Byng's[1] sentence is at last determined, and it does not appear, that he is likely to have it changed; perhaps His Majesty don't care to grant a reprieve, for fear of the people who are so violently incensed against him: I believe he is the first of his rank upon record, who has suffered such an exemplary punishment; the twelfth Article of War you see has determined his fate: I reckon this will put mettle into all his brethren of the navy, who (it may be expected) will perform wonders, whenever they are put to the trial.

Hendred March 19 1757

Dear Sir,

I have just now finished a great job of thatching; which is as much pleasure to me, as it may be to some great folks in having finished a fine building; indeed it has cost me above £7, and I had such another piece of work this time twelve month; so that I now hope that part of her premises is done for my time; I shall every year have something of this sort to be done, but nothing like this: it has been upon my mind for some years, as I knew it was what must be done sometime or other, but now I think we are in such a condition that (if I was to die tomorrow) no dilapidations could possibly be demanded. As to our garden, I think the last snow did not make so much alteration as I thought it would. Our snow drops and crocus's were not much the worse for it, and now they look very pert and lively all over the garden: the winds have been very high this week, but I know of no harm they have done in our neighbourhood; I see by last night's papers, that there have been accidents in Town, particularly Mr. George Pitt's coach being crushed to pieces and his coachman almost killed, by the fall of a stack of chimneys.

Your letter came to me just in that ragged condition, in which you have received some of mine, the cover was held but only by a piece of the main seal; upon talking with the postman who brings them from Abingdon, he tells me it can't be avoided; he has seen several so upon opening the bags that come from other parts; for they have a way (he says) at the post houses of girding them up close in the bags one upon the other with leather belts, and in order to press them together, they stamp hard upon the bags when they draw the belt together; so that we can have no redress I believe.

Hendred April 19th 1757

Dear Sir,

The death of the Archbishop, you see, has made a great motion amongst

---

1 Admiral Byng (1704–1757). Defeated off Minorca and shot for neglect of duty, despite a strong recommendation to mercy by his Court Martial.

the troops of the ecclesiastic state; it is said, and I suppose with good reason, that our Bishop is to go to York; so that we shall have a new Bishop as well as a new Dean; the latter was a schoolfellow of mine at Eton, though no intimate acquaintance, and the Bishop that is to be (Thomas) I knew very well some years ago, when I was a lecturer in Town; but perhaps he is now too great to know any thing of me: though Bishop Gilbert goes to York, he may still be of some service to me at Salisbury, whenever a canonry is vacant, as he has the command of the whole chapter, (except the new Dean) and has now provided for all his relations in it; I believe I shall put him in mind of me, if ever I should see a vacancy, though he be at so great a distance: you see that the Duke of Grafton is recovered of his late illness; I thought it not improper to write a letter of compliment to His Grace upon the occasion, which I sent about a fortnight ago; such letters as these you know are unanswerable.

My wife and I (I thank God) are both well; but the two little ones have some humours in their blood, which is pretty troublesome to them at present; Binney's shows itself about the ears and George's in his legs: he has always had a violent itching in his blood at this time of the year, and makes himself quite bloody with scratching, when he's half asleep: but sometime ago, he happened to beat the skin off his heel by a board, which not being minded got to be a sore, and when it was almost well Binny trod upon it, which made it worse, and then he had a violent humour fall into it; but now it is almost well; though as he has now got this itching humour come upon him with the warm weather, we are afraid it may make him bad again; but we intend to give him some physic next week; he is very brisk, and never complains (even when it is dressed) but only restless with itching o'nights. We hope the fine weather is now set in for some time; our garden looks the better for it, as I suppose yours does too. My wife desires to know how the china aster is to be managed; and pray let us hear whether you have seen any thing of your mountain ash, for ours do not appear.

Hendred June 18th 1757

Dear Sir,

We have had great riots at Abingdon this week, on the account of the dearness of corn; the mob rose and siezed a large quantity of corn and flour that was on board a barge, and carried it off, in spite of the magistrates; they likewise plundered the butchers, and threatened going further; but I hear the gentlemen of the town have sent for a party of soldiers from Wallingford to suppress them. Another party of them were in readiness at Wantage a few days ago, with a design to seize some wheat that they heard was coming to town; but the owners having timely notice of their intention never brought it: the necessities of the poor are great without all dispute, and there is a fault somewhere in keeping up the price of corn; but notwithstanding this, the sufferers are not to be judges of their own cause, and thus to set themselves up as redressers of the grievances they sustain; no one's property can be safe, if they are suffered to go on at this rate, without opposition; for people of this stamp will be guilty of all manner of depredations, if they find they can go on without punishment: I hope therefore some method will be taken, to put a stop to these tumults, not only in our parts but every where else: besides, they make matters now much worse than they otherwise would be; for if people's properties are to be thus disposed of by an unruly mob, the farmers who have any corn, will be afraid to bring it to market, and consequently the price will rather rise than fall.

My sister Charlotte's account of our *pressing* letters to my mother, is a little overstrained: she has several times talked of coming down here for a few weeks in the summer; and then we thought it proper to give her a formal invitation; but for fear the whole family should be so obliging, as to give us their good company all together, we thought proper to hint at such an inconvenience, and invite only the two greatest strangers, who were my sister Nanny and little Becky. We had a letter last post from Charlotte, but not a word about their coming; and I find they have taken it into their head, that Jack has told us his whole love affair; for she calls the Lady by her name, which is Monins; and tells us the second time, that she writes a good hand and good sense, as appears by several letters wrote to Charlotte, who seems to hug us herself much in the prospect of such a sister: but I don't hear a word of her fortune, or her family; so that I am in some fear for the noble captain, lest the articles of capitulation should not turn out so much to his advantage, as I could wish. We are afraid we are going to lose our good old neighbour, Mr. Wymondesold, who is dangerously ill at his house at Wanstead; he is attended by two physicians, and it's thought he can't recover: he will be a great loss to this neighbourhood, as he does a great deal of good, and with great discretion and judgement.

July 16 1757

Dear Sir,

I find both by yours as well as by letters from Axyard, that you have had your annual visitants; they seemed vastly delighted with the entertainment you gave them, and say they never saw you look better, and in more spirits; my aunt too I hear is pure and well, and you were all pure and merry together — "Mr. London was so kind as to read us several things of his own writing, and it's a thousand pities he was not bred to one of the learned professions, for he would have made a good figure in any" — you may see by this, that every body have [sic] the same way of thinking with regard to your abilities, men, women and children; your neighbour the good old Doctor has said the same to me more than once; to which I shall only add this wish — that the Church of England was every[where] supplied with clergy, of as good abilities and as good principles.

My mother is very compassionate, and has a great deal of christian charity; I only wish she had a little more British coin, to answer these good inclinations for doing good; a larger fortune would not be greatly misapplied I verily believe: I am sorry to hear, that my brother Tom has no better a regard for his word of honour; I think he uses her ill; when I write to him again, I shall take notice of what you say, though I am apt to think it would have more weight with him, if it came immediately from you Sir, as he perhaps may take it into his head, that I never write but when I have some fault to find with him; as indeed that has often been the case.

I fancy, if my mother takes any journey this summer at all, it will be to visit my brother Jack in camp; for as he will now be within a day's journey of Axyard, it perhaps may be thought more adviseable to take a little pleasure there, than to break of the frequent intercourse between the Camp and the Town, by making a stay at Hendred. As we have no great reason to think, that we shall see them here this summer, notwithstanding they seem to say that a fortnight's time will fix this visit; my wife and I intend the week after next to go to Mr. Penyston's at Cornwall for two or three days, as we have had much invitation there for some time, and this week we had another letter about it; so we intend not to defer it any longer; as we go through Blenheim Park, my wife will have an opportunity of seeing that famous pile of building. The weather has been hotter this last week than I have felt it for many a year; the wheat comes on bravely with it, a little rain would be of service to the other corn, and to the fields that are mowed; our grass has run short hereabouts, and hay is very dear, but it is very good. Our garden looks very white, and our grass quite russet, things come forward too fast, we can't eat peas and beans fast enough: we have had great quantities of strawberries, and very fine ones, gooseberries and currants in great abundance; but our walls will bear no fruit but plums, of which we have too many; for they are most unwholesome fruit of all I think, and I am always glad when they are gone; for the children eat but too many of them, and there is no preventing it. I think we have some of the finest lettuces we ever have had, and are obliged to your garden for them; for they are from some seed that William sent Joe. I am obliged to you for your kind wishes, in wanting me nearer to you; it is what I have often wished myself, for I think verily we could contrive to be no bad company together, as we have both (to make myself no ill compliment) pretty much the same way of thinking: but, though perhaps we don't foresee any inconvenience that might attend either of us, upon a nearer situation, yet undoubtedly there would be in some respect or other, or our lot had not fell at so great a distance asunder; therefore this and every other bar to our supposed happiness must still remain as it is; and we must rest contented, by thinking it to be (as it really is) the best condition for us to be in: for with regard to our concerns in the natural world, that proposition of Pope's is infallibly true — whatever is, is right — though it will not hold good as to our moral concerns.

My wife and I have now been acquainted for somewhat more than twenty five years; and I think she appears more lovely in my eyes now, than she did this day nine years: for she is like some sort of flowers, which are pleasing at first sight; but are of that modest nature, as not to discover the richness of their colours, till they are viewed with some attention; and then their beauties rise to the sight upon every examination; our two little name-sakes are both pure and well, which adds greatly to the pleasure of this anniversary; George is a very good boy, and begins to be something of a grammarian, Binny goes to a Dame's school; and as a specimen of her proficiency in that branch of learning, she is going to knit me a pair of garters.

I have now got to the end of my tether, and shall conclude with all our duties to your self and my aunt, whose healths we did not remember to drink particularly last Thursday sennight, because they come in course every noon and every night; my wife and I being such formal sort of folks, that we never take our glass after meals without wishing health to Ditton, as well as all our other relations.

                                                  Hendred Aug. 13 1757

Dear Sir,

I have had the same lamentations from Axyard as you have had; and my answer has been, rather letters of congratulation than of condolence; by showing them the consequences of this departure, that it is the surest step to a Company — that the true spirit of a soldier rejoices at such a time as this — that hope gets the better of fear — that future promotion engages all his thoughts — and that Providence more particularly concerns itself, in behalf of those who act bravely for the honour of their King and Country: I wrote to Jack yesterday something in the same way, with a word or two about the young lady at Dover, the thoughts of whom would push him on to exert himself upon this occasion, in hopes of her and a Captain's commission for his reward when he returns. Your next article is Bishop Coneybeare's Sermons; I think (as you do) that they are very good and rational, but they are very long; and in my opinion he is too apt to labour a point, that wants no proof; his deductions are carried on in such a long string, that the understanding of the generality of his readers may perhaps be a little too much hampered in them: his style is by no means elegant, neither is his manner of reasoning so concise and striking, as Bishop Sherlock's: that which pleases me most of all his discourses, is the seventh of the first volume, upon the distinction of Rich and Poor; the length is the only objection I have to this sermon. I must now enter upon my own history for about this last fortnight; you must understand there is a vacancy at present amongst the canons at Salisbury: as soon as I hear of it, I wrote to the Archbishop of York and begged the favour of his recommendation of me to the chapter, as it must be his interest alone that can make me a new canon; I at the same time wrote to his brother Mr. Gilbert, to Dr. Dodwell,

and to Archdeacon Rolleston, (all three canons) and told them that I had
wrote to the Archbishop and hoped upon his recommendation I should
have the favour of their vote and interest: my neighbour the Warden of All
Souls was so kind as to back my request to Dr. Dodwell: in two posts I had
the Archbishop's answer, who told me, that "it was not *fit* for him, now that
he was removed from Salisbury, to interfere in what was to be done there,
but he wished me success". Soon after I had a letter from Dr. Dodwell,
who expressed himself very handsomely, and much in my favour, as he did
also in answer to the Warden, saying that he should be glad if the election
was to end in me; but that they were all obliged to act by the influence of
their superior in that church, or one who *had* been their superior. Upon the
receipt of the Archbishop's letter, I acquainted them all again, with His
Grace's resolutions, and hoped (as they were now at liberty) they would act
in my favour; and at the same time I wrote to the Bishop of Winchester,
desiring that His Lordship would second my request to Archdeacon
Rolleston (who has received most of his preferment from him). I had to this
a very honest answer, that he should have readily complied with my
request, if I had wrote a few posts sooner, but that another gentleman had
asked him to do the same thing; and he would give me the same answer, as
he did that gentleman, which was this — *if you are sure of the Gilbert
interest (who are Mr. Gilbert, Dr. Dodwell, Mr. Sherrard, and Mr.
Rolleston) you will be the man; if not, not:* since this I have had a second
letter from Dr. Dodwell, who writes very handsomely and very friendly,
tells me how acceptable it would be to him to have a man of my character
(as he is pleased to say) among them; but that they are all greatly
embarrassed how to act; he tells me sincerely, that if the Archbishop was to
name the man, I should not be him, for though (he says) he knows the
Archbishop has a regard and esteem for me, yet I should not be the first he
would name, as his brother in law and several others would be glad of the
same recommendation, but could not get it; I mean the Archbishop's
brother in law one Mr. Walton of Mitcham in Surrey: he says, he should
have been glad if His Grace would nominate his particular friend, but as he
does not, they must endeavour to choose him, whom they have reason to
think he will be best pleased with. By a letter to the Warden of All Souls
from a friend of his, I since find that the Archbishop inclines to Mr.
Hamilton a brother of Lord Abercorn's and it is supposed that he will be
the man at last, though there are some other candidates, the principal of
whom is the present Bishop of Salisbury's son in law. I have had a letter
from Mr. Rolleston much to the same effect with that from Dr. Dodwell,
wishing that I was to be the person, and as to Mr. Gilbert, I have not heard
from him yet; I know he has been from Salisbury, but I suppose it will be
much to the same purpose with the other two; so that I may now sit down
contented at Hendred, and enjoy what I have already: I can't but say, it
would be a very eligible thing; but my not succeeding will be no such
disappointment, as to give me a moment's uneasiness. I would not have that
mentioned again, about the Archbishop's changing his mind about this

election, for notwithstanding what he has told me, he does interfere in it, and for Mr. Hamilton; but I would not have it mentioned, for fear it should come about to him: for who knows what he may still do for me, though he don't care to favour me at Salisbury? What he has done already, was without my asking; and perhaps he had rather take his own way in conferring his favours: I intend shortly to write to him again, and tickle him up upon his refusal of my request. I shall likewise write to the old Bishop of Winchester, and thank him for the favour of his letter, for it is downright honest, without any art at all, and I like him the better for that: His Grace of York is a little too refined.

September 10 1757

Dear Sir,

The late bad weather come indeed at a time, when our farmers had just begun their wheat harvest; it put them into great hurry and confusion; they apprehended all their labour lost, and their corn would be good for nothing; upon this presumption the markets here have risen again; but to show how unknowing these people are, and how unworthy the blessings of Providence; the weather has since taken up a little at times, and they have had an opportunity of getting in their corn; and now they all acknowledge that it is the finest wheat crop they have ever had; and that the rain has done it a vast deal of good; nay had it not been for this weather, which they have so ungratefully murmured at, their wheat had been all spoiled, for it was taken with a blight, which the rains have washed off, and brought it to the utmost perfection, there being very little grown, and that only such as grew under hedges and in close places, they suppose that one with another ten sheaves will yield above a bushel of corn; some of it that was leased, has been ground, and makes the finest and whitest bread, that ever was eat; which is quite a treat to the poor people, who have fared but hardly: so that I think we have great reason to be thankful for what, but a few weeks ago we thought would be very prejudicial to us. My wife and I had a very pleasant day for our journey to Mr. Penyston's, but when we got there it began raining, and continued so more or less every day, till that on which we returned, which was fine enough over head, but the roads were bad: I showed my wife Blenheim, but it did not answer her expectations; nor indeed does it any one's who has seen many great houses in England; the furniture is but indifferent for such a house, and the paintings none of the best; the library and the chapel are the best apartments in their kind, that is to be seen in the whole building, the *elegance* of which is too well known to be mentioned. When we returned home, we found our little girl with the chicken pox upon her, it was just upon the turn, she was very well with it, and had been so all the time, except one day just before it come out and then she was a little feverish; she has taken physic three times, and is now pure and well: George came out with it on Thursday, but was no ways out of order, either before or since, except a little peevish a day or two before; so that I hope we shall soon get this affair well over with them both: our attention is at present taken up with the greatest concern of all, and that is the small pox, which we are now come to a resolution to let them have by innoculation; I fancy it will be performed upon them about Michaelmas, a physician from Oxford, whom we have consulted, will be over here next week, and then we shall fix the time: we are induced to it by the great risk they will run in the natural way, (which there is no likelihood of their avoiding when they go out to schools) and from that uncommon success, that this practice meets with everywhere, which I am inclined to think (from this success) is a method that Providence has been pleased to point out to us, for the avoiding of more danger. We have lost our worthy neighbour Mr. Wymondesold; he was brought down on Thursday from Wansted to be buried at Lockinge: according to his own directions, it was a private funeral, only one mourning coach, he was carried directly into church without pall bearers, or scutcheons: there were several rings given upon the occasion, one of which I have: he died at a very great age, eighty, and was one of the most perfect sensible men at his age that I ever knew. If poor Sir John had taken care some years ago, and had less to do with salt water places, he would not have had occasion to have such recourse to Brighthelmstone, and waters of that sort now: I am afraid he will find no relief any where, but what I can understand of his complaint.

Hendred Oct 5 1757

Dear Sir,

I have the pleasure to tell you, that our children are out of danger, the small pox is come out upon them both, and they are likely to have it very light; and the best (our physician says, who was with us yesterday) that ever he saw: they were pure and well all the time, till about Monday morning last, on Tuesday morning we saw something of them upon George, and yesterday they were out quite plump, he has a few in his face, and some about his limbs, though not many, the most are about the incision upon the arm, and fine ones they be: Binny was a day later than him, but she is not like to have so many as her brother, the surgeon says, who was here just now, and wished her joy of the worst being over: but they have had no symptoms at all, but what are usual and regular; and I have not had a moment's uneasiness about them: if one could possibly have made choice of all the circumstances of this distemper, it would have been natural to have taken those, which have attended it all along: and I think we have great reason to be thankful to God for these great mercies. My wife has been pure and well, and very easy all the while; she is at the Archdeacon's where I send her an account three or four times a day; our servants are at a blacksmith's just by; so that I have only the blacksmith's wife and the Clerk's wife in the house with me, and very good company we are all together, for we eat and drink at one table, which makes the less trouble; and very careful women they be, which was my reason for asking them to come, who don't make a practice of this nursing. The children have innoculated and bleeded all the dolls and things they could lay hands on, and have made us laugh very often at their odd conversation.

Hendred Nov. 17 1757

Dear Sir,

Your last favour I received by Sunday's post, and am glad to hear that you and my aunt continue well: we are now all got together again[1], after above six weeks separation, which you may judge is a matter of no small joy to us all, to my self in particular it is, for I was but half alive during my confinement: I have taken all the precaution that is possible, and hope that we shall feel no ill effects from anything that is past: what you have said in your last upon this subject, is very judicious, and has its weight; but as the business is now well over, I cannot say that I ought to repent of what has been attended with such success; and I hope that neither my self nor my children may ever feel any bad effects, from what was at first undertaken with a good intention, and carried on with a sincere trust and confidence in the good providence of God, and with continual prayers to him for the success, that has followed: as to my having a different opinion of this practice sometime ago, I own it is true; nor did I change it upon any conference, that I have had with my neighbour the Archdeacon: but it was greatly owing to Dr. Dodwell, who is the greatest advocate I know; and what I had heard once from him about two years ago, ran much in my mind, till I was confirmed in my resolution of putting it into practice.

The latter season, as you observe, has been extremely fine; our garden has been a beauty to the very last: grapes we have had in great abundance; but as we have not taken that care as you do, the frost has hurt them pretty much, though there are several bunches still upon the trees; cauliflowers too we have had till this week, and very fine ones, as well as lettuce and as good radishes as in the spring of this year. Corn and butcher's meat are still very dear with us, and I can't think the reason of it, considering the plentiful crops we have had this year.

Dec. 24 1757

Dear Sir,

We had the favour of yours last Sunday, and are very glad to hear that Mrs. Croft is so happy in the recovery of her children. My wife indeed had some thoughts of writing herself; but being at present a little wanting in proper

---

1  N.B. We met all together on Thursday at dinner [Woodward's marginal note]

materials, for such a composition, she hopes my aunt will give her a little credit, till she can pick up something, that may be worth her reading. As to you and I Sir, I think we at present must not plead this excuse; for the brave King of Prussia seems, as if he would not only furnish out materials, for the correspondence of those who so much admire him as we do; but also for the subject of his history, which is so full of such uncommon incidents, and such unparalleled bravery and conduct, that posterity will hardly credit what we have the pleasure to know, for certain and undisputed truths. I had a letter last night from Axyard, with a barrel of very good oysters, which my wife and I tapped for supper: but as we had no body to assist us, you may judge we did not go very deep. I don't find that Jack is yet come thither, so his call upon you is still to be: I don't find but they are all very well; but not a word of public news do we ever hear from them. About a month ago I had a letter from my brother Tom by way of congratulation, which I answered by the next post, and gave him an invitation here as usual; but I have heard nothing from him since.

Frank the last<br>Hendred Jan 21. 1758

Dear Sir,

The article of mourning,[1] seems at present to be the great subject of female conversation in these parts, as well as yours: I don't see that any one puts himself to much expense about it; those who have any thing black in their wardrobes, put it on, and those who have none, dress as usual; as to ourselves, my wife has a Norwich crape, which goes on when we are from home; and I make an alteration in my self, with buttons and buckles. I don't find that the death of the Old Chevalier[2] is yet confirmed, I know it has been so reported; but a friend of mine at Oxford, who come from Town this week, told me yesterday, that it was not known for certain: this gentleman is lately married to a £9,000 fortune, daughter to a gentleman who was chaplain to the King of Prussia's grandfather; from whom I have had much account of that Kingdom, and of its glorious monarch in particular: he told me that his Lady dined one day, whilst they were in Town, at a merchant's who is himself a Prussian, through whose hands all the money has passed that has been sent over thither: he says, the day he dined there was Prince Ferdinand's birthday, where all the company were Germans but himself and two more: the dinner was very elegant, but all in German taste: he there drank the genuine old hock, that came from Heidelburgh, and as different as any thing can be from what is usually called so here in England;

---

1   Probably for the Princess Caroline Elizabeth, daughter of George II. She died on the 28th December 1757.

2   Only son of James II of England. Otherwise known as the "Old Pretender", from his pretension to the throne.

extreme good he says, and better than any wine he ever tasted: he told me the names of several dishes they had, but I can't repeat them. The conversation you may judge, turned chiefly upon the conduct of their great king, and every one strove who should extol him most.

I reckon by this time you have had your transient visit from Captain Jack, in his way to Town; for I understand he came thither one day last week: as to the American chief, I don't find there has been any news of him, since his letter received in October. My brother Tom I hear has been in Town, and behaved very well, by paying my mother four guineas, and also for his shirts; so that I think he acquits himself very honourably; and I hope he will always take care to do so: he threatens a visit to us in the summer. This frosty weather sets us much upon our legs, we were over at the Archdeacon's last Tuesday, to celebrate their wedding day, and as usual stayed there all night. Whilst we were there, we had an invitation to a gentleman's at Arnton about two and a half miles off from us, where we dined, with Mrs. Eyston and her sister Fanny, who came and returned after supper in their chariot; my wife and I walked home by moonshine. Your intercourse with Gerrard Street is very agreeable; but I think the ladies there reap the most advantage of it; for in my opinion a good basket of garden stuff, is worth twenty accounts of rackets, drums and routs etc.

Axyard, Feb. 28 1758

Dear Sir,

I had the favour of yours last night, when I come to Town, and am obliged to you for your kind invitation to George; but as it may be inconvenient to myself, and no great diversion to him, to take this journey, I believe he will be better satisfied with staying in Town, where every thing he sees will give him pleasure, therefore I hope you and my aunt will excuse his paying his duty to you both, till such time as he can do it with more propriety and satisfaction on all sides. We had a good day yesterday overhead, though somewhat too cold, but I don't find that we have either of us received any ill effects from it. I left my wife and Binny both well, who desired their duty. We found the family here all ready to receive us, except Charlotte and Jack, who were gone out two different ways; she to dine in the City and he to a rout, one came home before supper, and the other I saluted this morning at breakfast. You may naturally conclude, I had no great opportunity to exercise my faculty of speaking, as all the tongues of Babel have been let loose about my ears, ever since I have been here.

It is next to an impossibility to deliver one's thoughts upon paper, as one ought to do, in the situation I am in at present; for I am now writing in the dining room; and unfortunately for me the argument in dispute seems rather too warm; and by what I can apprehend the subject of debate concerns neither of the contending parties; but there seems to be a great division amongst them, some of them look upon Captain O'Hara as a man

View of Piccadilly, with Green Park on the left. This was the route of Woodward's stage-coach on his journeys between London and Berkshire

*(Museum of London)*

of great humanity, and the Rev. Mr. Parfait a very insolent ungrateful man; others oppose it, and change the tables exactly; the Rev. Mr. Parfait is a poor, unhappy man with five children, and Captain O'Hara is a barbarous inhuman creature, to treat a clergyman in such a manner; and trample upon him because he is in low circumstances: in short, the cause is tried with strong arguments on both sides, and great vehemence of speech; but there is such a constant volubility of speech, and such high rhetoric used by the Council on both sides, that I am at a loss (in my present situation) to sum up the evidence, and give my verdict accordingly; for they have done me the honour to call for my opinion more than once, which I have begged leave to waive at present, as I am not in a condition to take the merits of this important cause: the several advocates seem to be strongly affected with the circumstances of the case; and I have just lifted my head from my paper, to let them know, that in my own private opinion, it was hardly worth while continuing a debate of this nature, which by what I can collect from some scattering circumstances, did not seem to me to concern either party; but I am sorry to say, that what I have offered seems not to have the desired effect; for (if it be possible) the warmth of the dispute is increased: therefore it will be to no purpose for me to make use of my pen any longer.


                                               Hendred March 18 1758

Dear Sir,

Before I give an account of my journey from London to Hendred, I must let my aunt know what passed between us in Axyard, about her coming up to Town: I took an opportunity to introduce the subject, and said it was a pity she had not had the small pox, for she would be glad to be now and then with her daughter in Town, if her house was but safe; and indeed I had heard her mention something of business that she had to do in Town, but did not care to trust herself in their house: upon which my mother and sisters all together said — why won't Mrs. London come here? She knows she will be very welcome; didn't she say she would? I told them I did not hear her say she would, but I fancied she would not be displeased at such an invitation, because she talked of some business she had to do about Lady Day, which would require her being in Town for some few days: my mother replied — I am sure she shall be heartily welcome: so here we dropped the discourse; and I imagine my mother will write to my aunt, if it don't go out of her head again.

    I forgot to tell you, that in my return from Ditton to London, I took up an elderly lady at Hampton Court, who had come upon a visit to her daughters, as she told me; she was a very conversible, well bred woman; and had the remains of beauty: I found by her conversation, that she was a lady of property, for she talked of some estate she had at Fulham, and at Brentford: upon going through Twickenham, I took notice of the house where Lady Peachey lived; upon which she said — Ay, I knew Lady

Peachey very well, and her sisters too; pray Madam! says I, which of her sisters did you know? For I am a very near relation to one of them; Mrs. Woodward, Sir says she; — Madam! I am her son — upon which she turned and looked me in the face, and said that there was some likeness about my eyes: she said she visited her, when she lived in Aldersgate Street, and immediately asked me after my brother Charles and Richard, and what children my present mother had, for she had visited her once: I told her, and asked her if she knew you; she said no; but said that my grandfather London lived in a house of hers at Fulham once, and she believed Lady Peachey was born there: I asked her name which was Mason; but where she lived when she knew my mother I know not: we set her down at Brentford, and there I took my leave of her.

The day I set out from London was an extreme fine one; our company was only a dirty man and his wife, with a rough dog at the bottom of the coach, and a large crop eared cat in a bag, who sat between his master and mistress: they talked high of a sister of the gentleman's, who kept her coach; and seemed to set a value upon themselves, for this equipage of a collateral branch: by their own appearance, it seemed as if they had all their household about them; I found they were anabaptists. They told me they were going to live at Wallingford, — that they had never been five miles out of town before — that a friend had taken a house for them, with coach house and stabling for eight horses, which would be very convenient when the rich sister came to see them, whom they seemed to expect in about a fortnight, for she could not help being greatly concerned at their parting — that their goods were to come on Friday, though they knew not of going away till the day before, when their friend's letter came to tell them of the house he had hired; and they had been all the afternoon packing up with the assistance of five porters: the gentleman was indeed the most dirty, stinking fellow I ever saw, a very rough beard, and a glass eye, which he was always wiping with a nasty blue and white handkerchief. By several inconsistencies in his talk, I took him for one who could not live any longer where he was, but was obliged to retire to a friend's in the country: when we came to Wallingford, they marched off to their friend's, with the cat and dog, and five small parcels, one of which was a single quart bottle, and they called it wine: great enquiry had often been made after a hamper of wine, which was supposed, by mistake of the porter, to be carried to the waggon. George and I, when we had dismissed our companions, sat down to a dish of tea, and after a good night's rest set out the next morning for Hendred, where we found all well; Binny had been out of order with a cold, but is now well; Joe has a cold and a rash, as Binny had, but is getting better. My wife and I yesterday drank tea with the Archdeacon, who is upon the mending hand.

Hendred April 15 1758

Dear Sir,

The extraordinary account you give me of the poor old Doctor surprised us much; the old lady must certainly be very whimsical, or mad, which is not many degrees beyond; I hope by this time he is safe underground; for if I was in Pennicott's place, I should not have been well pleased, to have had my house filled so long with the noisome stench of a carcase; it may require some fumigations to get rid of it: I reckon you hear by this time, how he likes his habitation, and what demand he may have made for dilapidations for certainly there is great room for such a demand. We are very sorry to hear, that Mrs. Croft had such a bad time, but hope she is now got well again: as to her troubles on account of her servants, it is a vexatious, though not uncommon case, particularly in and about London; it is an order of our species that we can't well do without; but there are but few of us, who have not reason to complain of them: my wife and I both join in our compliments to them both, and heartily wish well out of her difficulties. I imagine my aunt may by this time have made one at the fire in Axyard; where I can easily figure her to myself, sitting in the attitude of a hearer, whilst the loud orators of Dover Court are endeavouring to entertain her all at once, with their respective stories: her head seems to be in a constant motion, by addressing it to the several speakers; her great good manners frequently prompt her to make some reply, but I see it is impossible; for the current of the opposite stream sets in too hard against her; so that she is under a necessity of being silent, whilst nods and smiles supply the place of all her answers. George went to school last Monday sennight, very courageously; Joe and I attended him; I dined at his master's and left him very well satisfied; the Friday and Saturday after I saw him again, as I went to and as I returned from Oxford, and all mighty well: I sent a small parcel to him last Monday with a letter; and he sent me an answer by the post, his own inditing, and a very good one for such a young scribe. One of our parish happened to see him on Thursday, and I hear he is very well, and don't want to come home; so that I think we have a good point gained: he is somewhat missed at home, from whence he never was before without one of us; but that wears off by degrees: the two old folks are so simple, as to talk of fetching him home for they are supposed to have some small regard for the lad: poor little Binny seems at a loss for her play fellow; but we endeavour to make up that matter as well as we can with her, by taking her out a walking with us when the weather is fit: but indeed at present it is very unpleasant.

We have had a terrible fire this week at Farnborough, about five miles off, which has done very considerable damage; all the stables, barns, outhouses, ricks of hay, and wood piles, together with seven good horses were entirely consumed; the man I know, he's a very substantial farmer, though a tenant, and his loss, (besides the landlord's who is rich enough) will amount to above £300: my wife and I were up there the day after, to see an acquaintance of ours, who was greatly terrified with a fire so near her own house.

Hendred Sept. 2nd 1758

Dear Sir,

The affair of Louisburgh, (as you observe) has been matter of great joy all over England; the public are informed by every paper, what sort of reception this good news met with in different parts of the Kingdom: but as you may have not seen the rejoicing upon that occasion, in any of the public papers, that were made here at Hendred, I will transmit the account in writing. We had the news by the Sunday's post: and as our chief politicians are always impatient for news every post night, I immediately sent it to them, at the blacksmith's hard by, where the committee generally sits for the dispatch of business: the worthy members immediately rose, and adjourned to the belfry, to which place I also sent them a bucket of ale, with the healths to be remembered: the whole parish was soon got together, and the bells struck up; more liquor was given by other inhabitants, and all the guns in the parish, that had been employed in frightening the birds from the corn, were collected together; and with these they fired in repeated volleys from the top of the tower: in short, nothing was heard almost the whole night long, but huzzas, firing of guns, and ringing of bells, to the no small amusement of those, who were not inclined to sleep: some other villages in the neighbourhood, who were not so early in their intelligence of what passes in public, thought the town was on fire, and were coming up in great numbers to our assistance; but being better informed, retired back again, with a full resolution to have the same rejoicings the next evening, at their own parishes; and accordingly they had: you may see by this, that we can rejoice as heartily as others of His Majesty's subjects, though we don't choose to put ourselves to the expense of illuminations.

Just after I wrote to you last, we had a visit from Mr. and Mrs. Pennyston, who called upon us for a few days, in their return from Farnham; and they brought with them a fine haunch of venison, as a present from Mrs. Manwaring, who is her sister; it was the largest and fattest I ever saw; and since that we have had one from our neighbour Wymondesold, as good as the other; and as his venison is not confined to his own table, we are to partake of a haunch of it at the Archdeacon's next Monday; so that you see, Sir, we are in very high feeding at this season, which is a sort of diet this part of the county has not been much used to, till my neighbour stocked his park; and now we meet with it at every house. My wife and I last Monday went over to Oxford, upon a visit to Dr. Kelly and his Lady, which had been promised ever since they were married; he has a mighty good house, and we were most agreeably entertained whilst we stayed, which was till Wednesday morning, and then we returned home to dinner. We called upon George in our way, and had the pleasure to find and leave him very well; his master gives a very good character of him and I hope he deserves it; both him and his sister grow very much, and are in good health. I fancy by your account of the alterations, Mr. Pennicott will make his house a good agreeable habitation; I am glad to find that you and my aunt are likely to have so good neighbours of them. You tell me of a good second crop of hay, that you have stacked up; I wish I had done the same; we are now seeing what we can do in that way; it is an experiment that never was tried before at Hendred; but if we have fine weather to make it, I hope to get a little together, which will be of good service, now that commodity is so dear.

Hendred Sept. 30 1758

Dear Sir,

I find by your last, that you think venison is proper diet for epistolary performances; you think mine ought to have been larger considering how well I had fared: I cannot say that I have made this observation; and am rather inclined to agree with Mr. Pope, who seems to think, it generally has a quite contrary effect; that this sort of food is apt to damp the genius, and be a clog to the superior faculties of the mind; his words (if I mistake not) are these —

> The soul subsides and wickedly inclines
> To seem but mortal ev'n in sound divines

Pope's Epit.

So that I think there is some merit due to me, that I could perform so well, after being so hard loaded: to speak the truth, I do not think this high way of living is of any great service, either to the mind or the body; for a proof of which we need only read some of those heavy pieces, that are now and then produced by some pampered author of high station; or take a view of their half-begotten offspring, if they happen to have any. And indeed, to show that the body is more improved in strength by a contrary way of living, I can at this instant produce you from the parish of Great Hendred full thirty instances; for I heard this morning that there are thirty women with child, who are the painstaking wives of some labouring men, and have had no other bread for this twelve month, but what was made of barley and beans, all fellows that are worked, and fed too (you see) like horses: so that in short, if we don't provide other sort of food for them, the parish will be over stocked with children. I have some thoughts of writing a treatise upon this subject, showing the prolific virtues of this sort of food, with reasons for encouraging it particularly in times of war, when there is likely to be such a consumption of men. I intend to recommend it to some friends of mine in this neighbourhood, as well as other places, who I know are in want of children; and if you thought Mr. John Peachey would not take it amiss, you might venture to prescribe a course of beans and barley to Sir John. My

Lady perhaps might not dislike the experiment. Since I heard of these wonderful effects, I have been thinking with myself, whether this was not one reason, why Pythagoras never suffered any beans to be brought to table at his school, it being (he supposed) too stimulating a diet for his scholars, and might be the cause of some misbehaviour in the young gentlemen and ladies, for (if I mistake not) he kept a boarding school for both sexes.

Hendred Decr. 30 1758

Dear Sir,

My wife and I are both extremely sorry to hear of the accident that has happened to my aunt, but hope that she will now soon get well again: I know very well what the condition of a person must be that has had such a wound; for I have experienced it my self, some few months before I was married, by a large garden bench slipping out of my hands, and the lower bar — scraping down one of my shins; I immediately washed it with rum, and kept the hot cloth on for some time, which made me almost mad with the pain; this by degrees assuaged the swelling, and other medicines being applied I got well though after a long time: but the best thing upon such occasions is, (what I have since tried with great success) red wine made hot in a spoon, and dabbed upon it with the piece of scarlet cloth as hot as you can possibly bear it, the cloth is left upon the leg to keep the stocking from it: it is an extreme painful remedy, but it is infallible; for it prevents all inflammations, and checks the humours that would otherwise have recourse to this opening: I don't mention this, as thinking it may be of service to my aunt now, (though if I had been with you, I would have prescribed it at the very first) but as a sure remedy, if any one should have the like accident, of a broken skin. We had the same account from Axyard, about the preparations for the bride and bridegroom, as you had; but as I am no connoisseur in the ladies' dress, I was obliged to take notice of some particulars, and desire an explanation; which I afterwards had from my sister Becky very much to my satisfaction: I have not yet heard of the arrival of these noble visitants, but I suppose it will not be long, before they make their entry: I would give a good deal to be in the next room, at the first interview; I dare say, as soon as the introductory ceremony is over, they will all be as great with our new sister, as if she had been bred and born amongst them; it will be *my sister* perhaps the first night, but I'd venture a good wager, that the next day they'll call her *Kitty*, the same familiar term of speech, that is always made use of by them, whenever they have occasion to speak of her: this was a point of decorum, that I took the liberty to dispute with them, when I was last in Town; but they carried it by a great majority of voices. We have been in expectation of my brother Tom's annual visit, as he had told us sometime ago, that he intended to eat some minced pie with us; but we have neither seen nor heard from him: I hope the poor fellow is not ill, that he has not wrote to us, because he has generally sent his excuse if he did not come. We are now in the midst of our Christmas feastings, and taking our rounds at one another's houses, Great Hendred being the only place in this neighbourhood, that keeps up this good old English custom; fowls and bacon, roast beef and mince pies, is the entertainment to be met with at every house, and the evening is spent in a game at five farthing lieu. Next Monday is our farmers' tithe feast, which is but a troublesome time, and I am always heartily glad when it is over; for it's very disagreeable sitting for half a day amongst such sort of folks, in a cloud of tobacco, attending to the price of corn and fat hogs, and almost stunned with the noise of their rustic mirth.

Hendred Jan. 27 1759

Dear Sir,

The weather is certainly very fine and pleasant, but far from healthy, at least about us, numbers of people continually dying of a most uncommon fever; for they lay a long while with it, and in a raving condition; few recover; it is quite terrifying to all the neighbours, as we are informed particularly from Abingdon: upon which account I am obliged to keep George at home a little longer than usual, last Monday being the day he should have gone: frosty weather is the wish of all people here-abouts, it being generally thought that such a season would be of service to purify the air, and make it more healthy than at present it is: we have had some few die of this fever in our own parish, but not many: our own family I thank God are very well. Your account of the mad dogs is a dreadful story; and Mr. Crowe I think has good reason to reproach himself for his obstinacy, for no one can say what the consequence may be, considering how long the dog was suffered to live amongst them all; I think verily, were it my own case, it would make me almost crazy; I hope your dog has been in no danger, or rather that he is dead; for I should never be easy, if I had the least suspicion of his being infected; I sometime ago hanged a favourite of mine, purely upon suspicion, for I was not sure she was bitten, though she had been in some danger of it. Your Reverend neighbour and his Lady are great vagrants, by the account you give of them; and I think (as you do) that it would have appeared better in the eye of his parish, if he had kept his Christmas with you, and given his neighbours a specimen of his charity, as well as of his hospitality: but as he is not so complaisant to you the first winter, there is but little reason to think he will be so hereafter. With regard to Mr. Pocock's character at Reading, I am informed he is a great swallower of drink; he has had one wife already, whom I once was in company with at a friend's house in Reading; her father was a bookseller and stationer there, his name was Mickelwright, concerned principally in the Reading Mercury; it was supposed he died rich; Miss being an heiress was snapt up by this Mr. Pocock, (who I think was then in some other business) as his new wife was fond of a cordial now and then, he was such an indulgent husband, as never to refuse her such an innocent amusement; it is supposed he took his share with his Deary; who happening not to have quite such a strong head as her spouse, he had the last glass and saw her drop first: whether she has left him sufficient comfort for so great a loss I know not; I once heard, that it was thought they lived too fast, but I can say nothing positively: if this second lady has the perfections of the last, the gentleman may stand a chance to make his fortune by matrimony. As you have heard from Axyard, I reckon you have been made acquainted with what has lately happened there — how the noble Captain and his Lady had contrived to raise a young recruit, who went off soon after they came to Town; it was well for the Lady she was in such good hands, and not at country quarters; otherwise she might have gone off too. We thought that we should have seen nothing of my brother Tom this Christmas, but he is now here with us; he had been in Town for about a week, and then came down to us; I understand he is to return to Axyard again, when he leaves Hendred; for as he happened to come there just at the time of all their confusion, on account of this dissaster, he had but little of their company, and was forced to smoke his pipe down in the kitchen; so he is to go back again, in order to be better entertained I suppose: he looks very hearty and well, and desires to join with my wife and I in our duty to your self and my aunt: he just came time enough to partake of four Christmas dinners; so now we have finished all our festivities.

Hendred Feb. 17 1759

Dear Sir,

The distemper which has been so much complained of in our parts of the country, seems to be pretty well over; so that I shall send George to school again on Monday; what might have been the cause of it, I know not, but it has been very fatal to several; and yet I understand, not only from you but also from Kent and Sussex, that the people in general were never known to be so well, as they have been this winter. Our parish, as well as yours has lately been in great confusion, on account of a mad dog, who passed through and bit several; but they have hanged them all; two men in a neighbouring village were likewise bitten, and are gone down to the salt water. My brother Tom left us yesterday, and is gone up to Axyard again, where he proposes to stay about a week, and then return home; he says that he hates London above all places, and would not live in Axyard, if they would give him his living there, they being in such a continual hurley burley from morning to night. As Mr. Pennicott is so frequently abroad, I suppose his church is supplied by a resident curate; otherwise he must trouble his neighbours pretty often, or neglect his duty; either of which are circumstances that must naturally lay him open to the just censures of all his parishioners: when his buildings and garden are complete, he may then perhaps reside more amongst you, and show himself another man than he seems to be at present. The situation of our public affairs at this time, must naturally rejoice the heart of every man, who has a love for his country, and any regard for its dignity; for we seem now to act with the true spirit of our forefathers, and our enemies are thoroughly sensible of it: for my own part, I have an uncommon pleasure, when I compare the present character of our great statesman,[1] with that which he once had at Eton school; and think with my self, that the same person, whom I have so often seen a boy playing at fives in the cloisters, is now the only one who has been able to bring our affairs to this happy crisis; and is every day planning schemes, that in all probability will raise us again, to the highest pitch of all our ancient glory: the execution of these schemes must naturally be attended with great expense; but no one sure will grudge that, if we gain the point that we aim at.

Hendred April 6 1759

Dear Sir,

The good appearance of the famous Kitty Fisher,[1] seems to engross the whole conversation of the Town; I had heard a good deal of her just before your letter, though not with such particulars: I understand, that it is the club at Arthur's who support her in this luxurious manner, many of whom have wives and families, which is a shocking consideration, and a glaring characteristic of the immorality of the present age: I hear she highly affronted the Duchess of Grafton, by refusing to give place to her at the play; and the next day Garrick spoke to her about it, and told her, he must insist upon her not appearing in that part of the House, for several ladies of quality made objections to being in her company; to which she replied — that she was surprised they should make that objection, for though she had not the honour to know them, she was perfectly acquainted with their husbands. I understand, that Sir John Peachey is going to the southern parts of France, which I suppose is no news to you: but you'll wonder perhaps how I should come by this piece of intelligence; and you'll wonder more, when I tell you I had it from a blacksmith: a man of this business in my neighbourhood has a daughter, who lives with Sir John, which I did not know of till very lately, when Joe told me, that he had been asked by this person, whether I was not a relation of Sir John Peachey, for his daughter had told him I was. As to the family in Axyard, I think they are not so respectful to you, as they should be, by neglecting to answer your letter: but they are in such a continual hurry, that I verily think such things slip

1    Pitt the Elder (Earl of Chatham)
1    Kitty Fisher. Immortalised in the nursery rhyme
      "Lucy Lockett lost her pocket"
      "Kitty Fisher found it"
      "Not a penny was there in it"
      "Only ribbon round it".

their memory: it is the same with us; we have had a silence for almost a month, when we have wanted an answer; and then comes a bed roll of excuses about going out and coming in, bad heads, business, washing and ironing and God knows what, all which is to be made amends for the future: last night I had a letter, by proxy, from my mother, who is but *so so*, all in a hurry scurry, the Captain and his Lady being to strike their tents, and decamp this week; where their next quarters are to be, they don't say, but I fancy not quite so commodious as the last.

Hendred June 23rd 1759

Dear Sir,

I must now let you know, that we are going to have an addition of one more to our family here at Hendred: a lady whom my aunt has seen, is coming to live with us, Mrs. Price of Lockinge, she has had a very handsome legacy left her lately; and intended to quit the place she was in before, the person she was with having had a paralytic stroke, and not so capable of accommodating her, as she used to be: she had frequently given hints to my wife, of her great desire to be with us, if we thought it would be agreeable: at last she spoke out, and my wife mentioned it to me; so we have agreed upon terms, and shall have her with us in about a month's time: she is a very easy, agreeable woman, and we shall like one another, I fancy, very well: she is to live just as we do, and we are to find her in every thing but washing; the price she is to pay is £25 per annum, which I believe is not amiss either for one or the other: she was very well satisfied with the prospect of her new habitation: she will not only be an agreeable person to us at all times, but also a good companion for my wife, whenever I have any call from home; and as they are very suitable to each other in temper, and in their ways of thinking, there is a great friendship between them, and I fancy we shall all think ourselves the better for each other's company.

I suppose you may have heard of my mother's jaunt to Richmond lately, upon the affair of a wedding, where my sisters were bridesmaids by the account I had of it, they spent a very jolly day; my mother and some others came back to Town that night, and my sisters were left behind to see fair play between the combatants; the lady is an old acquaintance in the family, and a very good fortune; she is very well married, and I hear sister Becky is going out of Town with them for a few months this summer, to a house of hers in Northamptonshire.

Axyard Thursday Morn 7 o'clock<br>1759 Sept 27

Dear Sir,

I am now set down to give you an account of my self and my proceedings,

since the morning I left Ditton: William I reckon gave you an account of
Mr. Pennicott's post chaises and that it was thought, the party that were
going upon the secret expedition were to rendezvous at his house: Mr. &
Mrs. Berkeley, for fear of being too late, had come out without their breakfast, and when I came into the house at Kingston, were enquiring after tea
or coffee; but a dirty girl, who had conducted them into a dirty room,
throwed a large dirty cloth upon a dirty table, and could produce nothing
more than the third part of a loaf and a piece of butter, of which they took a
few mouthfuls, and paid only six pence for it; the same damsel brought a
bunch of keys to Mr. Berkeley, and asked him if they did not belong to
him, which he immediately acknowledged, having dropped them by some
means when he come there last Saturday from Town; he asked her if they
had found a guinea, which was answered in the negative, for upon pulling
out some papers from his pocket, I understood he had dropped such a
piece, either in the stage coach or in that house; but he was forced to go
away without it. We then proceeded from Hampton Wick, where we took
upon a gentleman; and though I did not at that time take much notice of
the house he came out of, I found that he lodged where Miss Peacheys do,
and had done so there four years; he appeared a good sensible knowing
man, a great friend to Pitt and the King of Prussia; for the old lady renewed
the conversation we had at Mr. Pennicotts, and the gentleman and I were
her opponents, she is really a clever old lady, and has read a great deal,
understands something of Italian as well as French; and by my having to
quote a piece of Latin, in a story I was telling them, she immediately took
the sense of it, just as I was going to explain it to her: our subjects were
various, and she spoke sensibly enough to them all: we dropped them at the
upper end of the Haymarket, the gentleman went on towards Fleet Street,
and I was set down at a wax chandler's in Charing Cross; and pray let my
aunt know the name is Coggs, where I enquired after the candles she
ordered me; I saw some of ten in the pound, which I fancy will suit her
purpose; if she has a whole pound they are 2s.10d., if less three shillings:
the woman of the shop looked hard in my face, and asked me if my name
was not Woodward, I told her yes; I thought Sir I knew you again, says
she, for I have often heard you with a great deal of pleasure at St. Martin's:
a speech of this nature is not easily answered, so I bowed and thanked her
for her good opinion of one, who so little deserved it: I told her the enquiry
I made was for a friend of mine, who would send to her shop for some of
her candles. When I came to Axyard, I found them all well, and much
enquiry was made after my brother and sister: — a stranger being there it
was asked whether my brother's CHARIOT brought me to Kingston, I said
yes. Though all here are angry with me, because I don't allow my self more
time in Town, yet when I have contrived matters so, as to spend the chief
of it here with them, they at the same time are frustrating my design, by
filling the house with so much company, that I have but little opportunity
of conversing with them except it be in public; and indeed it is hard to say
which is the most disagreeable, to talk in a room full of people where there

St. Martin's church, Trafalgar Square. A shopkeeper near Charing Cross
complimented Woodward on his preaching there years after the event

*(Museum of London)*

are no hearers, or to have one's own private chat frequently interrupted by altercations, and uneasy janglings; for in my life I never saw so much as there is here, upon the most trifling matters, which can be no great entertainment to a person, who is only a visitor, and has no concern with the dispute. The evening I came, we were to spend at a neighbour's, Mr. Guarin's, who are old acquaintance of mine, so that was agreeable enough; yesterday was laid out for the Cornwallis's family at next door, who were to dine and spend the evening, I went out in the morning, and did not return till twelve, and met Mrs. Cockran in the dining room; soon as she was gone, in came a Captain and a Colonel and his wife, who were much pressed to dine, the lady stayed; presently comes Mrs. Bowker, she was lately married where my mother and sisters were; she was asked to, but did not stay; besides others running in and out till dinner came upon the table; so in great hurry and confusion yesterday was passed till near twelve at night. This is the whole account to the present time, in the afternoon at five I am to call upon Dr. Betty, and the evening in Axyard is to be spent with another set, in honour to me. Saturday noon I set out for Hendred, and am very glad of it. I had a letter yesterday from there, and they were all well. I cannot pick up one scrap of news for you: the only topic is Lord George Sackville, who is universally condemned but most people think no further notice will be taken of him, at least not yet awhile.


                                                     Hendred Oct. 6th 1759
Dear Sir,

The account of my self, after I sent away your letter by the Thursday's post, is very insignificant, for I can only tell you, that I lost sixpence that night at cribbage, with some friends out of Southampton Row, who came on purpose to see me, a good natured man and his wife; she had formerly been a silk mercer's wife in my parish, when I was Lecturer at Friday Street church, and after her husband's death, was married to the present gentleman, who belongs to the Custom House; he is an intimate acquaintance of Mr. Wymondesold my neighbour here. The next day was spent at home, and in the evening a family game at four handed cribbage; about ten I set off in a hack for the Black Lion in Water Lane, (the very best inn in London, as private as any country house) where I lay, and took coach the next morning at five for Hendred: my companions were, two small women and a very corpulent man, by profession a cider merchant, but (as I told him) he seemed by his size to have dealt in more generous liquors than cider, for he was one of the largest I ever saw; in Piccadilly we took up a woman and a little girl, who were going to Wantage, and I had some knowledge of them: as we came over Hounslow Heath, we saw a gentleman in a white flannel waistcoat, walking very fast, and soon afterwards we understood, that he was walking for a wager of twenty guineas to Reading, Lord Caernarvon having laid him that sum, that he did not walk to that place from London (which is but thirty nine miles) in sixteen hours; but I have since heard he did it in less by four hours. I got safe to Hendred between six and seven, and had a very pleasant day for travelling; I found my wife, Mrs. Price, and all the family well, and were very glad to hear, that I left you and my aunt so at Ditton. You may naturally think, that I took the first opportunity of talking with my little women, about your kind endeavours for us, with regard to Sir John's living, and it gave her great pleasure; but as women are naturally good at contrivances, she is of opinion, that in case we should ever come to have the offer of it, our best way would be to get an exchange of Hendred for some other living within a proper distance of that, so as to hold them both; and this I fancy might be done; for I suppose any gentleman possessed of one of £150 per annum would not dislike to exchange that for Hendred, which is £210; so that by such a contrivance as this, I might live at Stedham my self, and put a curate into the other: and then if I live long enough to see George in Orders, perhaps I might be allowed the favour of signing Stedham up to him, and so by that means get him well provided for, during my own life: these are schemes that we have been forming to ourselves; but whether they may ever succeed, depends upon many contingencies: however there is nothing amiss, by indulging ourselves in these imaginary prospects of our future welfare, and that of our children; such sort of pleasure will do us no harm, provided we don't build too much upon it, and leave but room enough for a disappointment.

Hendred Dec. 1st 1759

Dear Sir,

I am very glad to hear, that Sir John continues so well as he is, notwithstanding his lameness; and wish he may be able to recommend Dr. Barry to others, for the same disorder; but as he has tried so many physicians, and been subject to so many different regimens, there is but little hopes of success, particularly in a weakness of so long standing. I am much obliged to the Ladies in Gerrard Street, for their kind expressions with regard to me; and shall take it as a favour, if you will please to let them know at all times, how sensible I am of their friendly regards. I shall take an opportunity of mentioning to my sister Charlotte, what you have said to me about her visit to Ditton; I think (as you observe) it may be best to defer it; for undoubtedly she will have an inclination to return, when Harry comes to Town, as he is so great a stranger to all the family, and is not to stay in England longer than March they say. Jack I find is marched to Farnham, where he takes up his quarters, perhaps for the winter; it was a little unlucky for him, that he could not stay to see his wife brought to bed, who I understand expects it every day; but this is one of the hundred and fifty inconveniences that attend a soldier's marriage. Mrs. Price, who is with us, is much in her own chamber, except at meal times; and indeed she is a very good woman, but does not much contribute to Society; for she has lived so long by her self, that she is not much cut out for a family way; somewhat formal and particular in her ways, and very ceremonious upon all occasions; no great lover of company; and not at all given to any sorts of amusements, such as cards: which is in the first place owing to her education, (for I find she has been bred amongst Dissenters) and at present there is some difference between her and her sister's husband, who are jointly concerned in an executorship; so that her affairs, upon this windfall, are not settled, which makes her more low spirited and out of order than she otherwise might be: so that at present we have not that enjoyment in her, as we expected, by way of an additional companion.

                                                                    Dec. 22 1759
Dear Sir,

I was very glad to find by your last, that the sharpness of the weather has had no bad effect upon you; for I was observing to my wife, that you have born it as well as any of our farmers, who all allowed it was as cold as ever they felt it abroad, and that the house was the best place: as to my self, I took the opportunity of going above ground, and walked about to see my friends at a distance; it being (as I always tell every body) the best time of the year to take such physic, for those who can bear the operation. The wind is now got about to another quarter, but not quite in the point for intelligence from Hawke: you was right in what you said, I had not then seen the account of Hawke's victory, my paper not coming till the evening, after your letter was sent to the post, it was a very fortunate event; for notwithstanding the great strength he had with him, there were great disadvantages against him; he was near a coast that he was not acquainted with, the wind setting towards it, and the night coming on apace; so that it was the greatest chance in the world, that he found good anchoring ground, otherwise he and all his ships might have drove ashore before daylight: I think it was something providential, that they were all preserved in the midst of so many dangers, they had to struggle with. I am afraid by your account that I have but a sorry kinsmen of that young Sears; for it is very surprising, that a man of his fortune should let his own mother's reputation suffer so much, even with her own brothers and sisters by his not complying with their just demands. What you tell me of the Governor and his young man, is not much to be wondered at, for I once knew just such another case; a natural son of Colonel Farmer was taken notice of very early in life, by his brother Sir Harry of Se'nake, who out of regard to the Colonel then dead, intended to bind him out prentice to some trade; but he soon altered his mind, and sent him to school and the university; bought a good living of £400 per annum for him, and thought to raise him by that means; but when he died he left him not only that Living, but his whole estate; the young man chose rather to be the country gentleman; he was so for some years; but when his estate was gone, he took refuge in the Church, where he continued his extravagance, and his Living is now sequestered for the payment of debts: whether this will ever be the case of the other gentleman, I pretend not to prophesy: but let things work on, and we will wait the event. I am sorry to hear poor Sir John is got so much worse, as not to have the free use of his hands; it is bad for himself and somewhat unlucky on account of his friends, to whom he might now and then give a helping hand. George came home yesterday; and by the little talk I had with him in the evening, he appears to be full as foreward as can be expected; and knows a great deal more than I did at his age, which I take to be owing to a better method of education than was the vogue at my time: I find he has got a little acquainted with geography, as well as other things, which his master instructs the boys in; by which means he will have a better taste for the books he reads, where the sailing of ships and the march of armies are described; I am very much pleased with the progress he has made; as he has very good parts, a quick apprehension, and a great lover of books, I am in hopes he will be no disgrace to his family.

Frank the last    E. Hendred Jan 14th 1760

Dear Sir,

I understand by a letter from my brother Jack, that his regiment is talked of for one of those who are to go abroad; he hopes it may not be upon either of these naval expeditions that are fitting out, but rather into Germany, as he has no chance of rising higher, he says, whilst he is in quarters at home; and I think he judges rightly, for no man should be a soldier, who could put up with the poor satisfaction of being a Lieutenant all his life time: Jack writes us word, his wife has given him a daughter at last; my wife and I had promised him our assistance, one or other of us, at the christening; so he now wrote us word of it, to put us in mind of the engagement; and as it is a godmother they want, my wife is to be one, and my mother (I suppose) the other; for he tells us, he intends to call her Mary Albinia, in honour of the two gossips; and the damsel has been so very complaisant, as to make her first step into public upon my wife's own birthday, which was the 7th of this month; so that Jack and his daughter have been mightily civil and polite, one in giving the name, and the other in coming into the world upon the birthday, of her godmother. I don't hear any thing more of Harry, so when he will come to England now, is very uncertain. We have had much to do with our Christmas neighbours but it is now almost over; though I dont find it has made any alteration in Mrs. Price; for she either went home just after tea, or did not go at all, being the most unfit person for company I ever saw in my life, formal, precise, and ceremonious to an intolerable degree; we never thought, before she came to us, that she would be so troublesome, as we find she is, for which reason we shall not continue together: we had agreed at first, that if there was any inconvenience found on either side, we were to be at liberty to mention it without any offence so I have taken this liberty (as she happened to give me a fair occasion about a week ago) and told her, that I found more inconvenience in a boarder than I was at first aware of, and as our ways and hers are so very different, it was not likely we should live together in that harmony, as perhaps might be wished by both parties; for she is very particular in her hours, and her ways of eating, not being fond of either hashed or broiled meats, with several particulars, which makes it very inconvenient and disagreeable to my wife and I; and so very nice and whimsical about the cleaning of her grate, and other things in her room, that our servants' time is chiefly taken up with her business, especially in the forenoon: some of these I mentioned to her: I told her, I should always have a respect for her as a worthy good woman (for that I believe she is) but could not think of spending my life with her by way of companion in the same house: she acknowledged, that she might have some particularities, which she had contracted by living so many years by herself in a farm house, where all the family were at her beck and willing to gratify her in her several inclinations: but this I told her could not be complied with in such a family as ours; I only consented to her request at first, purely to oblige her as she so much desired it; but I found such inconvenience, that I must beg leave to have my house to my self. Indeed she had once or twice spoke to my wife in terms, that I thought were rather fit for a common landlady, than for her; which gave me some offence: so we are to part some time in the summer; and my wife and I are both glad of it, for we are both sure we should never agree well together: for we should choose a boarder, as one would a companion for life, they should have the same dispositions, as near as one could guess, with one's self, and both parties should be inclined to the same amusements and ways of living, one with the other, without any ceremonious restraint; and where things are not upon this footing, there may be a formal civility, but no cordial agreement maintained.

Hendred Jan 26 1760

Dear Sir,

With regard to our inmate Mrs. Price I fancy about Lady Day we shall part; she has made several overtures towards staying again, but we still continue in the same mind, and only put it upon the footing, that a boarder upon any terms is more inconvenient than we imagined it to be, and therefore we would rather be without one: as to the expense of the closet, it was built upon her account, but as she will have had so little use of it, we think it but reasonable to make some allowance for that: and as we are the first, who make any objection to our stay, we can't be justified (at least to our own consciences, though we shall be losers by the bargain) to suffer her to be at the whole expense: this I have mentioned to her, but she seems still to insist upon not being allowed any thing for it, as it had not been built but upon her account, so I can say no more to that at present.

Hendred March 8th 1760

Dear Sir,

What I mentioned to you about my uncle Elford, in the Antiquities of Westminster Abbey, is exactly as I told it, which I wondered at too, he is there only called Singing Man to Queen Anne: I fancy the inscription I saw on a stone at Windsor, was that of his brother, whom I remember when I was at Eton school; he belonged to the chapels both of Eton and Windsor; he once got me in at an Installation; I suppose I had mentioned to some of the boys, that his brother was my uncle, for which reason they used to call him my uncle; I remember he had a prodigious red, blooded face, and sang a very good bass. You tell me, that Charlotte was a whole fortnight, between the beginning and ending of her letter to you, and that the reason was she was taken with a stye in her eye; I wish it has not taken the whole family, for we have heard nothing of them for more than this fortnight; perhaps Jack's going abroad may have put them all into great commotions; my new sister may be so much concerned at parting with her husband, that they are forced to carry her out into the air, sooth her melancholy with the music of oratorios, and endeavour to direct her grief with parties at cards; in the midst of which necessary amusements, it is not to be wondered, that there is not time for writing of letters. As to Lord George Sackville — I hear his friends are in great pain for him: the other Lord I suppose will be condemned to death, there being no likelihood of his escaping. We have lately been alarmed with mad dogs in our parish; Mrs Eyston has hanged two, who were bit, two died mad, and she has two more tied up, as they are not sure whether they were bit or no; a little favourite parlour dog of ours was bit by one of hers, and I immediately had him hanged; and am determined to have no more dogs, for I never had but one at a time, but have always had ill luck with them; and it only gives one concern, when one is obliged to put them to death: a shopkeeper in the town was bit by one of Mrs. Eyston's dogs in the hands, and her butler was pretty much slubbered with him about the hands, which were a little scratched with some bushes; so for fear of any ill consequences, they both set out for Southampton, and have been dipped in the salt water; I hope no ill effects may ensue; her coachman and her maid had been handling the dogs too as well as the others, (for they at first thought something was the matter with their mouths, and did not suspect madness) but they have been to an old horse doctor in the neighbourhood, and I suppose he has given them a drench: this you may judge has been the topic of much conversation.

Hendred March 31 1760

Dear Sir,

We had a very melancholy accident happened in our parish on Saturday; a
poor woman subject to fits being alone in her house, fell with her face into
the fire, (though there was hardly more than one might put in both one's
hands) and was burnt to death before any body came to her; she was wife to
a labouring man, and has left one child. Our agreeable boarder leaves us
tomorrow: it is impossible to say, how very teasing she has been for this last
quarter, in order to stay with us; she will take no denial, but asks pardon
for her impertinence and is putting the same question in a week's time: ever
since I first gave her notice of our parting, she has strangely altered her
behaviour, every thing that came to the table was the best of its kind that
could be, and nobody lived in so pretty a way as we did; many fine
expressions of the greatest regard for us above any one else — that she
certainly did behave strangely at her first coming, and was guilty of great
rudeness, but it was owing to a lowness of spirits — that now she was got
pure and well, the air agreed with her, and if we would but try her, she was
sure we should be very happy together; we still answered no: even since she
has made preparations for moving, and some of her things actually gone,
she has still persisted in these importunities; it was but last Friday she
attacked us twice, and told us she would take up with the worst room in the
house, and raise her price, if we would suffer her to stay; I was so provoked
at such a mean speech, that I could not help saying to her, that if she would
condescend to lay in the cellar, and give me £200 per annum I would not
accept of it. Whether any thing more will pass between us before tomorrow
evening, I cannot say; but my resolution is still the same, for I most
heartily despise such a mean spirit: I once told her, that if she was in low
circumstances, and did not know where to provide for herself, the case
would be different; but as she had a fortune, and might live any where, I
could not help being amazed at such importunity: I find now, by speaking
of her to other people, who knew more of her than we did, that they don't
at all wonder at our not liking to keep her, they are only surprised that she
ever came here at all: but it is certain we were greatly mistaken in her: I
own I always looked upon her as a good, sensible woman, and easy to live
with, though I knew she had some little particularities, which I thought
would not affect the quiet of a family; now she is all for company and cards,
which is very surprising, for she knows nothing of any game, nor do we
ever play with her; but she asks people to play at picquet with her, and once
in the holidays sat down at a table with some young folks at whist, where
they only laughed at her: but this I suppose is done to recommend her to
company; and my wife says it is owing to me, I having once or twice
unluckily said, that I didn't like people who would not play a game at whist
or four handed cribbage; so now she is qualifying herself for society: as she
has paid for the closet already, I intend, when she talks to me about her
board, to let that go for her quarter; for I think it would be unreasonable to

make her pay for what she has had so little use of, and it would not look well to the world: in short I must be contented to be a loser by my experiment of a boarder.

Hendred April 19 1760

Dear Sir,

I find by your last, with regard to our late boarder, that both you and my aunt would have been inclined to have tried her for another quarter, to whose opinion I would always pay a just deference, and I must own, I always agreed so far with my aunt's sentiments in this matter, that I thought her quarterly payments would be very convenient, on account of my boy's schooling: but had you known so much of her, both from experience as well as the report of others who were better acquainted with her, than we were, (though we have known her some years) as we do now; I am persuaded you would have been as resolute in your denial as we were: it is very true, the worst part of the year was over; but I much question whether we should have had any advantage by her for the rest of it; because I found by her talk, that if she had stayed till about mid-summer, she intended to spend the remainder of the summer with her friends in Derbyshire; and this time would not have been reckoned into her board; for I forget whether I ever told you one mean thing of her, which she desired might be allowed in her bargain, (and this too after we had settled all other terms) it was, that if she was absent at any time for a week or fortnight, she might have it deducted; this proposal somewhat surprised me, but as I really took her for a different person than what I have since found her to be, I consented to it, as thinking she would make it up to us some other way: so that if we were to have her with us all the dead and expensive time of the year, and receive no advantage from her in the summer, it was far better to be without such a boarder and her deductions; and I am apt to think you and my aunt will agree with me in this sentiment: besides, what pleasure and comfort could we have expected from each other, when we must have been obliged to live so much upon the guard; for if she had stayed with us again, it would be binding her up to her good behaviour, and that would have been a great restraint upon her, and not such satisfaction to us, who could not be supposed to act with that freedom and intimacy towards her, as we formerly have, considering what had passed. She is a woman of no sort of resolution, a failing in her visible to all who ever lived with her; her own sister, who is married to a clergyman about four miles off, is perfectly sensible of this, and told my wife but last week (as they were talking about her) that she heartily wished her sister could fix somewhere, but she was of that very wavering disposition, that she was afraid she would not; as to her living with her, it would make her life very miserable, for though she herself might contrive to humour her well enough, yet she was sure her husband would not, for she had some particularities which would not agree with every body. So that, if her own sister (as appears by this) could not be happy with her; there is little reason to think others would. She is now seeking out about the neighbourhood for some family to board in, (for she will not keep house her self, though it has often been proposed to her by her sister and others) but I fancy she will not soon meet with one to her mind; for she has been trying at this (as we are now told) many years ago: the person she is now with, is the widow of a farmer, where she lived for sixteen years before she came to us; but as the woman gets on in years, she is now desirous of going somewhere else; though by the by this was never mentioned till very lately; for she always used to be commending Dame Smith (that is her name) and saying how happy she lived at Lockinge for sixteen years, and was afraid she never should be so happy again; but as soon as ever we talked of parting, Dame Smith was never more mentioned; and now she is seeking for another habitation. The night before she went from us, she made a very unlucky confession, by owning there was something of self interest in pressing so much to stay with us, for she could not but say, that she never could expect to live in such a family upon such terms; I only said, that I was sorry to find, that she could think of making the disquiet of our family subservient to such a principle. We at last parted very good friends, and I told her, we would come and see her at Lockinge, when she was settled, and should always be glad to do her any act of friendship, consistent with the convenience of my own family: we have met her once since at her sister's, but I believe she is very unhappy in her own mind, though she has no manner of reason for it, being a single woman and fortune enough to support her very comfortably.

I must now turn to another relation, concerning our own family: Joe and Sarah are going to be married, though I cannot exactly say when. They have mentioned their intentions sometime ago, but at the same time could not tell how to bring themselves to part with us. They are very desirous of still keeping their places, if we give them leave; and indeed they are both such good servants, and have such a regard for the interest of us and our family, that we cannot help being willing to comply with their requests; for they are now entering upon their fifteenth year, and I am pretty sure we shall never get two such in their places, who are so well acquainted with all our ways, and whom we could put such confidence in, for I verily believe there cannot be two people of more upright principles in all respects: and indeed just at this time, it would be very inconvenient to part with them, for our cook maid leaves us the 1st of next month; not that we have any objection at all to her, for she is a very cleanly, good servant but I find she has a prospect of advancing herself; therefore we would not be her hindrance: so we have concluded, that they shall stay with us; and if we find that any inconveniences are likely to arise from their having children, we have agreed to part; though I fancy (as she is between forty and fifty) there may be none at all: when the wedding is to be, I know not, for they intend to be asked in the church, and I have had no notice of it yet: but by some expressions that have dropt from Joe, I fancy it may be intended about the time Molly comes into this country, in her way to her mother; but this is only our conjecture. So much for bed and board. Since there never was finer weather, our roads are just as they be in the midst of summer; great shows for rain, which would be serviceable to the grass, but none comes. We are glad to hear that you and my aunt continue so well; and so do we; the two children have had a rash, George is returned to school, Binny is now taking physic for hers. Agues are much about, and my wife being a professed Sangrado[1] for that distemper, has multitude of patients, that come to her three or four miles round, and great success she has with her powders.

Hendred July 7th 1760

Dear Sir,

Had I been sure, that I should not have heard from you by last night's post, I would have contrived this letter to have waited upon you tomorrow, which (if I mistake not) is your wedding day; but even as it is now, I hope it will not come too late, to assure you and my aunt of our sincere congratulations upon the occasion; and of our best wishes for the health of you both, that you may enjoy together the returns of this day, many more years: I reckon the compliments of Axyard are paid in person; I had a letter from thence last night, but nothing was said of this journey, though a great deal of another, that I understand is to be taken into Kent at Michaelmas, where my mother and her family are going to reside for the remainder of her life: this is told me as a secret, Sir Richard Loyd and Mr. Baird (a neighbour of theirs) being the only persons, who are yet made acquainted with it, except the landlord, to whom she gave notice last Saturday, as she tells me in her letter, of her leaving his house at Old Michaelmas: so I shall be obliged to you, Sir, if you would not mention it to any of the family, for I reckon they will have the pleasure of telling you themselves: the place they are going to is called Downe, a little village about five or six miles from Westerham, about a mile out of the road from London to Tonbridge: I am told it is a good house with a pretty little garden, and a yard for poultry and hogs; it belongs to a friend of my mother's, she tells me, but who I know not, and for that reason she has it upon better terms than any other tenant; she proposes great comfort and satisfaction in this retirement; the only inconvenience I find, is the neighbourhood, being none but farmers and their wives; this is rather the reverse of their way of living in Town, and I am afraid will not agree with the constitution of the family; such a sudden change in their scheme of life, will be apt to hurt the quiet they propose to enjoy, and prejudice them against the country; a man who has been used to get drunk every day, should not leave off his liquor all at once; it's a

---

1  Dr. Sangrado, a character in the play Gil Blas, by Le Sage. Usually used in a derogatory sense.

dangerous experiment and will never answer the end proposed. As they are come to this resolution at last, (what their chief motives to it may be, I know not) I think it would have been better, if they had retired some years ago, when the cause was removed that kept them so long in Town, I mean the death of old Lady Winch: for this was given for a reason, why they would not remove into the country: had they gone to Chertsey, when you once recommended a house to them, I should think it would have been more agreeable, than where they are now going to; which is too near to Westerham, a part of the world that did not afford my mother a great deal of comfort and satisfaction: but they have their reasons I suppose for what they do, and it is no concern of mine. My mother insists very strongly upon my bringing my wife and Binny to see her, before she leaves Axyard; and I believe I must comply with her request; I did indeed propose carrying Binny up, when I come to Ditton, as she has never been, and has desired it every year: but now, as she is going so far off, I shall take my wife at the same time: I fancy it will not be till the beginning of September because I am to be at Salisbury the ninth Sunday after Trinity, which is the third of next month; when we come, if I find it not inconvenient to you, my wife and I intend to pay our duty to you and my aunt for about a week, and another week will be spent in Axyard, where we shall leave the little girl: in order to lessen the expense of the journey, I propose going to a friend's house near Reading in our own chaise, where we may be taken up by the machine, that gets into London by noon; and this will be cheaper than going by our stage, and baiting upon the road; the house we shall go to, is a substantial farmer, whose friends live in our neighbourhood, so that our horses will cost us nothing; and the difference between the Wantage stage[1] and the Reading machine,[1] is three shillings a head, besides not baiting upon the road. This is our present intention, but you will hear more of this before we set out. George's master dined with me about a fortnight ago, who gives him a mighty good character for his diligence and quickness of parts; a great deal of this is the usual incense offered up to a parent; but I am apt to believe it true enough with regard to George, not only from my own examination of him, when he was at home, but likewise from the impartial account I had from another gentleman, who was with his master; who told me he had heard his master speak of him to other people in the same terms, and had observed himself (as he has been down there sometime at the house) very busy in the school at his exercice, when the rest of the boys were at play: which is a great pleasure to me and my wife, as all parents love to hear their children well spoken of; but the pleasure is doubled, when there is reason to think they deserve it. My brother Tom was here for a day or two last week, and brought Binny a pair of gold rings for her ears; there was a sharp contrast between vanity and fear, but vanity at last got the better, and her ears are bored, and like to do very well.

---

1   Machine and stage. It is unlikely that Woodward intended to differentiate between the two.
    Both words denoted a stage coach.

[July 1760]

Dear Sir,

I had the favour of yours on Wednesday evening, that being our wedding day, we had the Archdeacon and his family (as usual) to spend the day with us; his following is not so large at present, as it sometimes is, having but two at home with him: he has lately been at Bath, to bind one of his children prentice to his son John, who is an apothecary there, and in good business: he has lately had a fine of £200 paid in from his Archdeaconry, which is a convenient thing to a man upon this, and several other occasions; he had another of these windfalls about four or five years ago, so that it has been a valuable piece of preferment to him. Last Monday the Judge came to Abingdon to hold the assizes; my neighbour Wymondesold is High Sheriff of the County, but did not make so grand an appearance, as was expected from a man of his great fortune: there was his coach and six, a coach and four, and a chariot and pair, besides the horse people, who were not so numerous as I thought they would be: I dined with him on Monday at his house at Lockinge with the rest of the company, two French horns blowing for about an hour after dinner: we dined about one, and between three and four set out for Abingdon; the High Sheriff, his chaplain, and two more friends were in his own coach; Mr. Price and his brother (two neighbouring gentlemen) were in Mr. Price's coach and four; I was with Mr. Clarke in his chariot, after which came a one horse chair with an apothecary and a country curate, followed by a squadron of horse: the horns blowed at every village, through which we passed, and all sides of the road were lined with spectators of all ages; we stopped at the town of Abingdon, and drunk tea and other liquors; then, upon notice of the judges being upon the road, we set forward about a mile beyond Abingdon; but as they did not appear, we were invited by a gentleman and some ladies, (who lived where we waited upon the Judges) to drink tea and coffee, which we did in a very pretty alcove in the garden, the French horns blowing all the while: as soon as the Judges were in sight, we got into the carriages and conducted them to the Town Hall, where Mr. Clarke and I left them, and returned home between eight and nine: I was much invited to stay the whole assizes, but it was monstrous hot weather, and more drinking likely to go forward, than I cared for, I made a very good excuse and left them to themselves. I had a letter from Charlotte the same post with yours, she goes to be interred in Kent with the rest of the family. I fancy they told you the name of the place they are going to, and you might forget it, or they perhaps did not write it intelligibly; for they tell me, it is Downe, a village within two miles of Farnborough. They talk of being there by the 10th of October, a sad time of the year to make so great a change in, from town to Country, and the neighbourhood none but farmers; I wish it may agree with them, and answer the purposes of their removal; I think as you do, it is a saving scheme, and hope it will prove so in the end: they will be greatly missed in London, not only by us to whom they were serviceable upon many accounts, but also by several others, who received much civility from them.


Hendred.<br>Aug. 30 1760

Dear Sir,

My wife and I went to Oxford last Tuesday, upon a visit to Dr. Kelly and his Lady, where we stayed one night, and returned the next day after dinner; it is now a full twelve month since I was at that place; in the mean time a fine turnpike road has been finished, to within a mile of us, so that I never desire to drive a better or a pleasanter way; great part of it runs through a place called Bagley Wood, which is now as agreeable and charming, as I once remember it to be intolerable and melancholy: at our return I found your letter, which I find (by a neglect not usual with you) should have come to my hands last Sunday. I am glad you are all well at Ditton, and hope to find you so on Tuesday the 16th of next month; for our route lies thus: on Monday the 8th of September we propose going to Sonning about two miles the other side of Reading, where we shall lay at a friend's house, and be taken up the next morning by the machine for London: Tuesday in the week following; (which will be the 16th) we intend waiting upon you and my aunt at Ditton, and to stay with you till the Monday following; we shall then pack up our things on Tuesday, and return again to Sonning on the Wednesday, stay there on Thursday, and get home to Hendred on Friday; because we think it but handsome to give our friends there a little bit of our company, as they suffer us to make use of their house for an inn; and at the same time we don't think it advisable, to put off our return to Hendred, to the very last day of the week, for fear of bad weather: this is the scheme of our journey, which I generally plan in this manner, before I set out: and then all other matters are regulated accordingly. My wife joins with me in our duty to your self and my aunt, and love to sister Charlotte, who is a very good girl, and I wish she was married to a good honest parson, for she seems to be cut out for one of us.


Sonning near Reading<br>Saturday morn 11 o'clock<br>[Sept. or Oct. 1760]

Dear Sir,

You perhaps may be surprised to see my letter dated as above, but if you have had the same weather with you, as we have had here and still continues to be, your surprise will be over: but I must first of all tell you, that we got into the machine last Wednesday between twelve and one, we had only one passenger besides ourselves, who was a little girl about twelve years old, and she and Binny fell into one another's acquaintance immediately, being as great together, as if they had known one another these twenty years, no ceremony or forms on either side; they were both provided with cakes, walnuts and pears, and as both seemed to like their fare, they travelled on very agreeably together: in going over Maidenhead thicket, we stopped and saw a little of the race, it being the second day of the races, which was some little amusement to travellers, particularly to Binny who never saw one before: the weather was very favourable all the way, and we got there to our friend's house about six in the evening: the next day was vastly disagreeable, with wind and rain, so that we could only get to a gentleman's house, which is just by, who desired our friends here to bring us; he is a man of fortune, and has a very good house, that looks down upon the Thames, handsomely furnished; with one noble large room fitted up with shelves from top to bottom, all full of books in various languages; for he is a great reader I understand, as well as a great sportsman; he is now confined to his room with a fit of the gout. I was afraid for my wife and Binny, in so long a journey, where they would be so much exposed to the weather in a one horse chaise; upon which account our friends have prevailed upon us to send the man home with one of the horses, and stay till Monday, which we are now resolved to do, it being quite dangerous to attempt such a journey in such weather: Joe I find has got a bad cold and swelled face, so his wife's brother came with the horses, and is now returned again with one of them; but he has a brother in this parish, who (very luckily for us) goes to Hendred next Monday upon his own business, so we are to have him with us to ride before the chaise, and carry our cloak bag. I suppose Mr. Pennicott might tell you, that he called at my mother's this day sennight, just as we were going to dinner; but I could not prevail upon him to stay, I was sorry my letter was sent to the post about an hour before he came: I saw him again (as I suppose you may have heard) last Wednesday, as the coach happened to stop in Piccadilly; he told me you and my aunt were well: sure he has something extraordinary in agitation, that his calls to Town are so very frequent.

Tuesday morn.

P.S:

We got home yesterday in the afternoon very safe and well, without any rain at all; but it was most sad weather all the while we were at Sonning; I hope both you and my aunt are now got better than when we left you; I remember you said, that you was sure some very bad weather was coming, by what you felt in your self; if I had but put more faith in your prognostications, I verily think I should have been induced to alter my scheme, and have spent some longer time at Ditton and in London, rather than have been detained so long at the place where we were: but I am very glad I am got home, and no body shall catch me again five miles from home till next summer. We found Joe got quite well again, and very glad they all were to see us safe returned; for by our not coming at the time of day they expected us, they were full of strange fancies, about accidents and such things.

Hendred Octr. 18 1760

Dear Sir,

I was sorry to find my letter from London cost you, so much more than it was worth, but think you did right in convincing the post master of his forward mistake: my reason for folding down that part of a single letter is, that it does not look so clumsy, as it otherwise would do; but since I find His Majesty has such vigilant officers, in that branch of his Revenue, I shall take care for the future, that my friends may not pay more than their due, on account of my decent folding up of my letters. The account you give us of poor Sir John is melancholy enough; and I don't much wonder at it, considering the relaxed condition he has been in for so many years; another fit of this sort in all probability may be his last. I hope you have made use of one of the fine days we have lately had, for the gathering your vintage, for the weather has been very unsettled, and you must catch your day when you can find it; I am glad to find your grapes promise so well; I don't pretend to know much of a vineyard, I fancy there can be none in England of the size, more complete and of a better sort than your own; and as this has been the finest season every known in England for grapes, it is impossible for any garden to exceed yours, which I believe in the very worst seasons is always superior to others; your soil and trees are both good in their kind, but that without proper management would be but of little consequence. Yesterday in the afternoon I called in at my neighbours, Mr. Clarke of Arnton, whom I have mentioned to you as one; who gives me leave to call him my gamekeeper; I there met with a gentleman, whose name perhaps you have seen in the papers sometime ago, when we had the misfortune to lose the Prince George man of war by fire; it is one Dr. Sharpe, the then chaplain of that ship, whose account of this dreadful catastrophe was published in the newspapers; he was obliged to leap out of the cabin window, and was taken up by a boat, that put him on board another ship; we had a good deal of talk about that and other sea affairs, and he appeared to be a very sensible well behaved man, and much of a gentleman; he is still in the sea service I find, and came from Quiberon Bay last month. I find the departure of my mother's family is quite uncertain, as to the time; the same was said to us (as has been to you) when we were in Town; and I fancy it may depend upon some money business, that is to be done before they go; for I found by my mother that she intends to discharge all demands upon her and her family, though it may be with the lessening of their fortunes after her death: I think they are in the right to come to this agreement; for it's much better to do so, than to lease their estate incumbered with debts, which would lessen it much more in the end: if I guess right by what was said (for it was only by way of hint) some part of the estate is to be sold.

Hendred Novr. 8th 1760

Dear Sir,

We were very glad to find, that my wife's ham proved so good; for we had the fellow to it, since we came home, which we were by no means pleased with, and much concerned we were on account of that we had carried to Ditton; but as you have given it such high commendations, we are now quite at ease; and think ourselves much obliged to you and my aunt, for receiving this trifling present in so kind a manner: I can easily figure my self, not only the chit chat at dinner upon this subject, but likewise Mrs. Brown's behaviour at supper, in treating the same; methinks I see her just finishing two handsome slices, my aunt helping her to another, she laughing, eating and writing her encomiums to you, all at the same time; you with a smile tell her, she must come and partake of it again, whilst it lasts, she with a simper and a nod assures you that she accepts of your invitation; and seems so well pleased with her evening regale, that she does not in her heart much regret the absence of the noble captain. I am glad to hear so good an account of Sir John, and I think your prescription with regard to his diet, may be of service to him; I hope he will follow it: I reckon Mr. James Peachey is in high spirits upon the accession of his young master; we shall see in time, I imagine, a great alteration amongst the State Officers; at present you see things and persons are like to be continued, as they were in the late reign: the vigorous measures we have taken for some time last past, by the advice of a very able minister, have had their effect hitherto, as appears from the distressed condition of the French. I hear of no complaints from Axyard, any more than you do; I fancy this sudden change in the government, so engrosses all their thoughts, that they have not time to talk of their own grievances. As to the condition of Jack and his wife, I think as you do, he had better not have been so much at home; for I am afraid he will get more recruits than he can provide quarters for. Mrs. Spry is gone up to Town, to put her youngest girl prentice to her daughter Jenny the milliner; and the youngest son is to go to Oxford in the spring with an exhibition of £20 a year; so I think by degrees the Archdeacon will dispose of his ten children to their advantage.

Hendred Decr. 27 1760

Dear Sir,

By a letter I had from sister Charlotte last post, I find she intends to accept of your kind invitation to Ditton, as soon as it is in her power; she seemed to be sorry that she could not make a longer stay when she was there last: but as sister Becky is now learning the art and mystery of obstetricism in St. Paul's churchyard, till she is out of her time Charlotte can't leave my mother. They have had a grand rout I hear in Axyard, upon the 15th of this month, on account of my mother's birthday, and it was whispered by the company to one another, that they never saw a person look so well at the age of sixty nine; I fancy this same whisper went round at a very late hour in the evening, when the good company's sight was somewhat impaired by the entertainment they had had; for though I am always very glad to hear my mother is in tolerable good health and spirits, yet I should be afraid she would think me not sincere if I was to make the same speech to her; for indeed I am far from being of their opinion, who think so, unless she is greatly altered for the better within these three months. George came home from school last Saturday sennight, and improves much both in mind and body; he is very much grown, and forward enough in his Greek and other things; at present he is reading the History of Tom Jones, (for he is a very great reader) and seems to be much delighted with it; Binny listened to it with great attention, being one of his audience in the kitchen, and is much pleased.

Hendred Feb. 2nd 1761

Dear Sir,

I reckon you have heard, that my brother Jack has lost his wife; I can't but say I am very sorry for him, as I am told they were very happy in each other; who is to have the care of the two children I don't hear, but I suppose they will be put into my mother's hands, at least for the present during their infancy. I don't hear a word of the journey into Kent; I wish they have not forgot that they have a house there: when I was in Town last, Becky showed me a large quantity of jelly glasses, salvers, glass candle-sticks, glass cups etc. for a dessert, which she has purchased very cheap, and pleased herself much with the great bargain she had of them. But I am afraid they may be rather dear in the end: for in all probability she will be induced to set them off in perfection amongst her Kentish neighbours; and by giving them a specimen of her good taste in conserving jellies etc. will put the good family to more expense in their entertainments, than if she had not met with so cheap a purchase. Our Archdeacon holds still very well, he is in lodgings at Oxford with Mrs. Spry, it being thought necessary for him to be near his physician for some time; but he has ordered him nothing to take, but only advises him to move about and see his friends; I fancy he is to be there about six weeks; his son supplies his church: Mrs. Spry's brother the Bishop of Oxford has lately had an estate of £1,200 per annum fall into him, for want of renewing in time; it had been well for this family, if the Bishop had not taken another wife by whom he has two children; though now as it is he will be enabled to do many handsome things by them.

Hendred Feb. 16 1761

Dear Sir,

We had a letter last night from Axyard, by which I understand Mrs. Croft made them a visit last Saturday in the afternoon, and was very well: till this letter came, I had not hear a word of *Downe* for some months, not that any mention was made *when* they should go, only Charlotte hopes to be better in health and spirits, when she gets there; as I find she and all the family have been much out of order, on account of my brother Jack's wife: I understand he was to leave them as yesterday; he was going back to Dover, but was ordered to Norwich upon a recruiting party, which may be of more service to him in his present condition, than continuing at the place which will always be reminding him of what he has lost; the two children I hear are there, one with the grandmother, and the youngest at nurse, which is best for them; for I reckon they will hardly think of saddling my mother with either of them, though they be nearer to her than the grandchild she has already under her care. I hear you have been so kind, as to give Charlotte another invitation to Ditton; and indeed I think a more retired way of life would suit best with her, as she don't seem to have a genius for hurry and parade; the whole family I fancy would be much better in all respects, could they bring their minds into a more rational scheme of living; they would find their account in it every way, but some are too young, and some are too old, to learn the art of living happily. On Thursday we expect my wife's sister Kitty here for two or three months; who has been upon a visit at Penton for about the same time, so I hope she will give us as much of her company here; I find by her letter, that my sister Strother continues pure and well and has had no symptoms at all of the disorder she had about three months ago. Mrs. Eyston and Miss Fanny drank tea with us on Shrove Tuesday, and eat a good deal of bread and butter, as (they said) they should eat no more till Easter; for I understand, on account of the mild season, their Lent is very strictly kept; Miss Fanny took leave of her favourite boiled beef and pudding, and by her way of speaking it was with some reluctance; it must be very expensive to such a large family; as all sorts of fish, both fresh and salt are extremely dear now, particularly in this part of the country.

Hendred April 18 1761

Dear Sir,

The talk of our troops being landed at Belle Isle,[1] is so often affirmed and so often denied, that the generality of people don't know which side to believe: for my own part, I can hardly think so formidable an armament as

---

1   Belle Isle: an island off the south coast of Brittany.

this, could be made only for such a place. I had an opportunity last Thursday morning, of making some enquiry about this expedition, from a gentleman of note, who was with me in the parlour for above a quarter of an hour; but I did not care to ask him any questions about it for reasons you will be a judge of by and by: you must know Sir, we had just breakfasted and the things taken away, my wife and sister being gone into the garden and I upstairs a little busy in my room, when one of our maids called to me at the room door, in these words — will you please Sir to walk down when you are at leisure — I having just before observed a neighbour's daughter come into the house, thought that she might have some business with me, so did not put my self in much haste; when I came down, I asked at the kitchen door in a loud voice who wanted me? The maid said there was a gentleman in the parlour, and upon my turning round, (the door being open) I saw a tall thin gentleman in boots, a gold laced hat and a cockade, in a dark grey frock with a star; a person of this figure so little expected at His Majesty's good town of Hendred, surprised me somewhat; the usual greetings being over I seated the stranger in the best part of the room, and was much at a loss to guess who he should be (for he never mentioned his name) he very civilly asked pardon for troubling me (as he called it) but came to know whether the Archdeacon was in the Country, for he had been informed in his way hither, that he was not; I told him he was; he had some business (he said) with him, about the repair of a chapel within the Archdeacon's jurisdiction, which admitted of some disputes, the charge of which lay between his tenant's and Sir John Stonehouse's; all this while there was no mention of his own name; upon which (in order to know it) I gave him to understand that I supposed him to be Lord Barrington, (not that I thought him a bit like him, but he happened to be the first that came into my head, and a gentleman of this part of the Country, besides the compliment of taking him for a lord) but he immediately replied — no Sir, *Sir John Mordaunt*[2] — this being a name that I was no stranger to, I judged it best to take the Duke of Cumberland for my subject, who is expected in our neighbourhood very shortly. Sir John told me he saw His Royal Highness at his house in the forest two days before, and he talked of coming soon: so with his and some other things the time was passed, till Joe came in from the Town, who (as I had told Sir John before) was to put him in his way to Little Hendred; and I dare say his appearance put that worthy family into a sudden fever, Mrs. Spry in the midst of her breakfast flying out of the room to change her cap and apron, her daughter Molly following her mother's example, and the poor Archdeacon, in the midst of all the disorders of a forsaken room, left to the reception of this uncommon stranger: as I have since understood, our maid who first introduced him, told my wife and sister when they come in from the garden that she believed he was a Duke, for he had something upon [his] coat that she could

2   Sir John Mordaunt (1697–1780). Commanded the land forces in an unsuccessful attack on Rochefort, 1757.

not well describe: the whole Town of Hendred were greatly alarmed, when he came through and made up to the parsonage; and much enquiry has been made, as I hear from Joe, by Mrs. Eyston's family and all the Town, who this extraordinary person should be: a neighbouring gentleman was with me this morning, who told me that he heard as he came along, that I had a fine gentleman with a star to see me last Thursday: so you see, how much an event of this nature furnishes matter of speculation, for a country village.

Hendred June 3rd 1761

Dear Sir,

We have had more rain within this fortnight, than has been all the winter before; and as it is unusual to have a good glut of it about midsummer, I hope what we have had lately, and what we now have at this present writing, may serve for that season: it suits well with the grass, and will make hay cheap I reckon, but the farmers think they have had full enough for the corn lands: perhaps these eclipses (one of which is this day) and the transit of Venus that is to be on Saturday next, may in some measure contribute to the weather's being so inclined to wet. I don't know whether you may have heard any thing lately of my mother's family, who have been parted for above this fortnight, Sister Becky, Niece Becky, a man and a maid being at Downe, my mother and the rest were to have followed in a few days; but she poor woman has been extremely bad, and is now at Mr. Cornwallis's (the next door to her late house) very much out of order; we had a letter last Sunday from Charlotte, who with a maid and sister Nanny are the only persons left in Town; all the goods have been gone this fortnight; Charlotte hopes my mother will be able to undertake the journey by next week: I find she had fatigued herself too much with the packing up, and I reckon the thoughts of leaving a place where she had been so long an inhabitant, together with other difficulties she may have had to get over, in order to clear her passage into the country, may have been rather more than she was able to encounter, considering her age and shattered condition of body: if she finds she gets strength by the country air, and holds out about half a year, I am apt to think she may live some few years longer, but by the accounts I hear from her, I much fear this moving will be only a useless expense: Charlotte tells me, she was then writing a long letter to my brother Harry, whose last letter bore date about fifteen months ago; I fancy by so long a silence, he will write no more. Last Saturday sennight we were surprised about noon, with the arrival of my brother Tom, who come to make us a visit, he stayed with us till the Friday after; but as it happened to be pretty rainy most part of the time, he was obliged to keep much within doors, which was not very agreeable to him, who loves air: he looks very healthy, though some years older than me, as appears by his motion, his face and his mouth, for he has but five teeth in his head; and though he has much difficulty to chew his meat, yet he is carnally inclined, and deals in nothing but flesh; pie and cheese and broth he has nothing to do with, the two former being his aversion; he would by no means make a good boarder for any one: but as to smoking and drinking, he is very moderate, a pipe a day is all he takes, and I am told by people of Farnham, that he does not drink in the manner he used to do sometime ago, and is well respected by the gentlemen of that place, which I am glad to hear.

Hendred Aug. 8th. 1761

Dear Sir,

I am very glad to find, that the late hot weather has not indisposed either you or my aunt more than usual: as to ourselves, I thank God we are tolerably well at present, but I have for this week or ten days last past, been in a great deal of pain with a rheumatic disorder, I set out for Salisbury with a cold about me, found a pain in my shoulders for some time after, but thought I had got rid of it, when I returned; but since that it took me again, and plagued me pretty much in my left shoulder, moving gradually down my arm; I got a flannel sleeve which I have on at this time, which has been of much service to me, for I feel but little of it now, and that chiefly just below my elbow; I take gum guiacum every night and morning, and clear rhubarb now and then, I took a piece last night, and hope by this sort of regimen (if I take no fresh cold) soon to get quite rid of it; but it has been very painful to me all the hot weather, and particularly in bed, though not so very bad, but I could sleep when I lay on my back, and could always shave myself and my head all over; so that though I have been in much pain, yet I fancy by what I have been told of others, I have not been so bad as some people are who have not the use of their limbs with it. There seems to be a great deal of business cut out for the months between this and Christmas, a marriage, a coronation, and a peace; all great undertakings, and I make no doubt but they will all help to increase the present glory, and future happiness of the English nation. I can't conceive how the ladies manage matters so well, as to be mistresses of that retentive faculty, which is so necessary upon these occasions, when they are obliged to be confined to a seat for so many hours: a coronation is certainly a sight well worth seeing, could it be with any sort of conveniency; but a person pays dearly for it, who is pinned down to his seat for eight or ten hours together. The Archdeacon's family are at present in great joy; one of their sons, who is not yet twenty, was last Monday chosen a Fellow of Merton College in Oxford, which is worth £50 per annum; a fine provision for so young a man, and whose father has ten children; I am vastly glad of it, as I heartily wish well to the Archdeacon and all his family. I have heard nothing from Downe since I wrote to you last; but I reckon it is a dismal situation in the winter, as you say it is; however, as you observe, if they can be contented with it, they may feel the advantages of it. I wish you and my aunt were but a little nearer to us, particularly at this time, as we have in the house as fine a haunch of venison, as ever I saw, which we think of eating with some friends next Tuesday.

Hendred Aug. 22. 1761

Dear Sir,

I intend to go from hence to Reading on Monday the 14th, get up to London the next day in the machine, and set out the day after in the Kingston stage for Ditton; I have some little matters to do in Town, either going or coming, otherwise I should get down to you on the Tuesday, as the machine will be in Town between eleven and twelve; but as so short a time will only hurry me too much, I intend to lodge there one night: I shall be with you on Sunday, and should be glad if Mr. Pennicott would accept of one sermon instead of two; for most of my sermons are written so small, that I am sometimes at a loss when I come to read them in the pulpit, and am apt to make some little bogglings, unless I take the trouble to write them out fair; some indeed I have written out at different times, but those I believe have been preached at Ditton already: however, if I find he is greatly distressed, (as in all probability he may be, the Coronation being but two days after,) I will assist him in the best manner I can. There's a family of our acquaintance in this neighbourhood, who are invited up to Town, to see this grand show, and I wish with all my heart that I was to be one of their company; for the place where they are invited to is a gentleman's house in the Old Palace Yard, who is above making any advantage of his apartments; and as these are his relations, they are to go there the day before, where they are to lie; so that they will see all that is to be seen with the greatest pleasure and conveniency, the whole procession being to pass just before the windows of the house: Such a situation I should like very much; but to sit in one particular seat for so many hours, as many must do, exposed to the night air and other inconveniences, I own I would not accept of such a place, if it was offered me for nothing. One of the Archdeacon's daughters, who lately came from London, told us a pleasant story of what passed between a friend of hers in Westminster and a lady of quality, who came to her house with another lady, in order to look upon some apartments that she was to hire for the Coronation, and in moving about she went up a very narrow pair of stairs, where some bed-chambers were and as she was there she turned to her friend and said — I can't conceive how these poor creatures contrive to creep up into their beds — Oh! says the gentlewoman of the house (who overheard what she said) just in the same manner, Madam! as you and other poor creatures creep into yours: in looking upon the rooms, the lady said she should like to have such a one, (pointing to one in particular) together with the other apartments below stairs; no Madam says the gentlewoman, I can't let you have that or either of the others, for this is all I have for my own family — why Madam (replied the lady) it may be worth your while, for I can tell you I shall bring a large quantity of provisions with me, and what we don't make use of will be sufficient for you and your servants too — Indeed Madam! answers the other, (who was a little woman, Sally Spry says, but of a good deal of spirit) I my self never take any one's leavings, and as to my servants, they eat no body's scraps but those from my own table; therefore if you should have more than you eat your self, I would advise you to take them away with you, for nobody in this house will have any thing to do with them: the Lady was so displeased with this speech, that she left the house, and went to get apartments at another. We had a letter last post from Downe, my mother is a little better than she has been, but can't get an appetite for her victuals. I find Mrs. Bowker is there upon a visit, (one that perhaps you have had them speak of, her maiden name was Dickson, and married about two years ago to a gentleman in the City by St. Paul's). She treated Becky and Charlotte last week with a jaunt for one night to Tunbridge Wells, where they met with all my wife's relations, and were civilly entertained by them, went one night to the ball, and returned to Downe the next evening.

Hendred Sept. 5. 1761

Dear Sir,

The day your letter went from hence I had one from Downe by which I understand, that my mother was then so bad, that they did not think she would out live three days; we expected to hear by the next post (as they told we should) that she was dead; but that letter said she was a little better, though far from being out of danger; and we have had several since, all which are in the same style, that she is rather better, but so very weak that she don't sit up for above three hours in the day, and has little or no appetite: considering therefore the condition she is in at present, I believe it will not be taken well of me, if I come so near as Ditton and not go and see her; but when and in what manner I am to get there, we'll talk farther about, when I have the pleasure to see you, which will be next Tuesday sennight the 15th of this month, as I propose being in Town that day by the Reading machine, and getting down to Kingston in the stage that evening, where I shall beg leave to expect your conveyance to Ditton: I hope by that time to get rid of a troublesome disorder I have at present upon me: though nothing near so violent as it has been, which is a purging; I am at present under a proper regimen for it, and hope soon to get the better of it; my bowels are naturally tender, but more so at present, for which reason I am very cautious about what is to pass through them.

The wind we have at present, and have had for so long, must be a great disappointment not only to His Majesty, but I reckon likewise to his future consort, both of them no doubt having a secret inclination to see each other; and it must naturally be a very disagreeable situation, to be kept in so long expectation; Her Highness will have this advantage, by her being detained so long, that she will be a little more perfect in the English language, than she otherwise would have been if the wind had been fair to bring her over at once: the splendour of the embassy, that conveys her to England, and the grand doings that are to follow upon her arrival, will be quite as astonishing to Her Highness I should imagine, who in all probability never saw any thing like this in all her days; and when she comes to consider, that she herself is the cause of this profuse magnificence, and festival solemnities, it is enough one would think to turn her brain; she must be more than woman, to support herself properly under so much grandeur. I should not much care, if I was a prebend at Westminster just at this time; for the papers say, that the Dean and Chapter will share above £8,000 amongst them, on account of the Coronation; a fine dividend truly! My neighbour the Archdeacon has escaped a fit this last change of the moon, which is more than he ever has done before; and as he continues pure and well, I hope he may have no more returns.

Saturday Sept. 26 1761

Dear Sir,

I hope William got safe home, and has given you an account of the roads, and of our late arrival at Downe, where I found my mother much as I expected by the accounts I had had of her, quite low and feeble, and her faculties in a very weak condition; I did not at that time see any immediate signs of death, and none of recovery; and since then, the apothecary has been here, who assures my sisters, that she is not in any present danger; that she may still live many months longer, and years for ought he can see to the contrary now: so that he looks upon her condition, as a common cold (for that indeed she has) and knows nothing of that load upon her spirits, that has been gradually heaped up, on account of her worldly affairs. Poor woman, she is greatly fallen away, and her senses at times not so perfect as they should be, very froward and peevish, and much given to cry; so that my sisters are quite at a loss what to do with her sometimes, for though they do what they can to please her, it is not to be done: as they have but one maid, and my mother so helpless, as to want attendance of one sort or another every minute, there is great confusion and uneasiness in the family, which (I can't but say) has been vastly disagreeable to me, and I shall be heartily [glad] to be out of the house. I understand she has made her will, since she was here, and desires to be buried at Downe; Jack and his three sisters are her joint executors, and all are left equally alike; Harry (if he returns) is to have a fifth part, for I find he is still alive, but by his extravagance is likely to give the family so much trouble, that they now wish they have never heard of him more; and reason enough they have, for he has drawn a bill upon my mother (which she has protested) for £70, and says if a peace comes and he is disbanded, he shall want as much again; and all this from a Captain whose pay is ten shillings a day, two horses and two servants allowed him; but they hear he is not only extravagant in treats etc., but plays very high, so there can be no end of such expenses: this account of him gave my mother a violent shock, as it needs must, and she has been sinking ever since. I find, whenever my mother dies, they intend not to part; they shall quit this house when their year is up, and hire one of a small rent within reach of the penny post, in order to transact their business, and not see London unless they are obliged to it; for they intend to discharge all debts whatsoever, (nothing of which is yet done) as soon as possible, and live as well as they can upon what is left: they seem to say, that my mother has concealed her affairs too much from them, but that every one shall be satisfied to the utmost farthing; and when that is done (by what they can guess at present) their income will be very strait, they seem to think not much more than £50 a year, which is strait indeed, and to me quite unaccountable: Jack is so generous as to tell them, he will give up all his share to them, and behaves to them in a most affectionate manner: poor things! I heartily pity them, and hope their affairs will turn out better than they expect.

                                                                 Hendred Octr. 10th 1761
Dear Sir,

I believe I told you, that I came from Downe in the Tonbridge stage, where I met with a passenger, whom I had some knowledge of; she was a milliner who has kept the Wells season for above twenty years, and knew my wife and all her family; so you may judge we had a great deal to say to each other, with regard to all our Kentish and Sussex acquaintance: we had a very pleasant journey to Town, where we got about three o'clock; and in coming through Westminster they were very busy in pulling down the scaffolds, and clearing away all remains of the late jubilee. I heard a great deal, you may imagine about the Coronation, whilst I was in Town; every one agrees in this; — that it was badly conducted, and by no means a precedent in all things for any that is to come after; much confusion amongst all ranks in the procession, several things either neglected or forgot, amongst others the Sword of State, which was obliged to be supplied by that of the Lord Mayor — that the Queen is not handsome, but altogether a very agreeable little woman — that the King made a most graceful, amiable appearance; and during the whole ceremony in the Abbey, behaved with the utmost decency and dignity, that can possibly be conceived; was more ready in every part that he himself was to perform, than any of the Bishops; and at the time of his receiving the sacrament (it being doubted by the Archbishop whether he was to take off his crown or no) he took it off himself, and laid it by with much humility, and unaffected piety: he is certainly the wisest, the greatest, and best monarch I ever heard of, and I wish no future squabbles amongst his Ministers may affect the good principles, which he seems at present to have in the highest

Charles Fitzroy, 2nd Duke of Grafton. Woodward hoped to benefit from the Duke's patronage, but also held him in genuine affection and esteem
*(National Portrait Gallery, London)*

perfection. That story we heard of the Lord Westmoreland's kissing Lady S. Lennox's hand instead of the Queen's, was not true; a gentleman who had it from my Lord himself, told me, that at his first going into the drawing room, to pay his compliments, there was nobody to introduce him, and he was at some loss to find out which was Her Majesty, till a person there directed him to her. I have brought home her picture, and that of the King; his is very like, and those who have seen Her Majesty tell me, hers has no bad resemblance; but I suppose this was taken in a hurry, to gratify the curiosity of the people, at her first coming amongst us; we shall have a more striking likeness in all probability, before it is long; and then I shall have one of them both for a frame, to keep company with my old patron the Duke of Grafton, in the best parlour.

My neighbour the Archdeacon has had another of his fits just before I came home, but is now very well again; it has a little discomposed the family, as they thought by escaping one moon, he would have lost them entirely.

Hendred Octr. 24 1761

Dear Sir,

I am greatly obliged to you for your favour of the last packet and am vastly glad to find, that Sir John came off so well, and that he is thought to have received benefit from this new operation; what effect it may have upon his limbs, I don't pretend to say, and hope he may be the better for it; but as to its giving him vigour, towards the disappointment of the Groom and his family, I much doubt it: indeed if these good effects should follow, several noble families would have reason to return thanks to Sir John, for being the first who made this useful discovery; and all the electrical operators would be in high repute, to the utter shame and confusion of the good old gentlewoman, at the Two Blue Posts in Haydon Yard in the Minories, where the INESTIMABLE PROLIFICK ELIXIR is constantly advertised to be sold, for the benefit of all impotent people of both sexes. In a letter we lately had out of Kent from one of my wife's sisters, we had a story which has given me great pleasure to hear, as it is the greatest instance of filial piety and brotherly love, that I have lately met with: there's a clergyman in Sussex, whose name is Lushington, I knew him when at Oxford; he has a small living and six children; one of them is in the East Indies, and now not twenty three, he was one of those who escaped with life sometime ago, out of the Black Hole at Calcutta; since that he has been much befriended by Mr. Clive, who contrived to fix him in some advantageous post under the Nabob, by which he has gained a pretty deal of money; and to show that his life was not preserved in vain, and to no good purpose, he has lately sent over £2,500 as a present to his five brothers and sisters, and a certain sum of money to purchase an annuity of £100 for the longest life of his father and mother, an instance of such uncommon goodness, and in so young a man, is not I believe easily to be met with in the memoirs of any modern family: I only wish my brother Harry was possessed of but half of his virtues. I believe I forgot ever to tell you, that I paid my mother the guinea you sent by me to Downe, and she desired I should thank you, saying at the same time that you was the most punctual man she ever knew. And I fancy I never mentioned the great doings we had here at Hendred upon the Coronation Day; there was a sheep roasted whole, and money given for drink, with ringing of bells all day long, and bonfires etc. at night; so you see Sir, we of Great Hendred are none of your little folks, when we have a mind to exert ourselves.

Hendred Novr. 24 1761

Dear Sir,

I was in some doubt with my self, as covers are so scarce, whether I should write to you or no at this time: but as I was not sure, whether you had heard of my mother's death, I thought you would like to be informed of it; about a week before she died, she was taken speechless and so continued for several hours; after she come to her speech, she seemed tolerable well again, asked several questions relating to her family affairs, and gave orders who my sisters should write to when she was dead, as she thought herself not long for the world, with several other particulars as they told us in their letter; afterwards she continued restless and in much pain for above a week, till the day before she died, and then she seemed quiet and easy and went off without a sigh; this was the 12th of this month, we had an account of it the 15th and no letter since, so when she was buried, I know not; but she was to be buried at Downe, as they told me when I was there, it being her own orders: my sisters have had a vast fatigue of late, poor girls! for they were not in bed for ten nights together, I wish it may not make them ill: As we get nothing by my mother's death, and have nothing for mourning, we contrive to be as cheap as we can, upon the occasion, my wife makes her crepe sash do again, which was worn for the King and Mr. Campion, and only makes her a yard wide stuff for every day; Binny has a new crepe coat, and George does with what he had for the King; for a second mourning coat for him, I have contrived one of mine shall do, and have therefore bought me a raven grey coat: this is all that we have done at present, and I believe it will do very well, for all that we aim at, is but to be decent upon the occasion.

By all accounts the Lord Mayor's show was the grandest that ever was; but there seemed to be wanted there, as well as at the Coronation, a proper officer to regulate the procession, for what orders were given seemed to be but ill observed, for there was a long delay at their landing, and great stopping of coaches, which not only made the procession very late into the City, but very much confused: however their Majesties (we are told) and their royal companions, were much pleased with the entertainment, and the day concluded with much satisfaction on both sides. How will the public amuse themselves next, I wonder, for all the fine shows are now over, triumphs for Victories, and a public peace, are the only things left to feast their imaginations with now: but what and when all this will be, time must disclose.

We are at present got into our winter quarters having not been out of our village for these three weeks; my wife works and knits till about eight, and then we go to cribbage. My little scholar Binny reads, writes and works, mama and I being her preceptors; I was very well pleased to see that tenderness of disposition, which she has in a very great degree, by her not being able the other day to go on with reading the history of Joseph and his brethren, for the tears which she shed in a most plentiful manner: her brother did the same some years ago, and they will not make the worse man and woman for it hereafter.

Hendred Decr. 5 1761

Dear Sir,

We are concerned to hear you have been so much out of order; but I did not apprehend that to be the cause of your silence, I imagined it might be owing to your not having any thing particularly to say at that time. We are all very well here at Hendred, and endeavour to keep ourselves so, by getting out about whenever the ways are walkable. I had a letter last Sunday night from Mr. Penyston, my mother's nephew, who expresses a good deal of concern for my sisters, on account of their present situation, and tells me he should be very glad to be of any service to them that lays in his power; and indeed as he is a very honest and a very able man, (as a barrister at law) it might not be amiss if they would give up the management of their affairs to him, if he would undertake it for them; for as they intend selling their houses, in order to discharge their incumbrances, they will stand in need of some person of experience and integrity, to assist them in such a business; this I have since told him, but at the same time said that I should not mention what he had said to me, to my sisters, till I had his leave for it; so I shall expect to hear from him again; I had a letter from them by the same post, who say nothing in particular of their affairs, only that they shall have a good deal of trouble, but hope in time to get out of it all, and that they are as well as can be expected: so I hope matters may not be quite so low with them, as they might think they would be sometime ago: I find they have hopes of leaving Downe by Christmas, but are not yet resolved where to move to. My mother poor woman! (as you observe) was in general a very valuable woman; and if nothing more was required of us in this world, but to do good natured actions with all the money we could get, and at the same time be regardless of any future inconveniences, I don't know any one person so well qualified for life as she was; for she certainly was a woman of good and generous spirit, of more benevolence than economy, and though of very good understanding in several respects, not quite discreet enough to know when she had done what was proper for her circumstances; so that what faults she had, they seemed to carry some excuse with them, as they were virtues in excess: I hope she will meet with her reward for her past afflictions here, and that none of her family will be very great sufferers, by any indiscretions of hers in the management of her affairs. There is a person lately dead in the neighbourhood, (at Molesey) who by his industry in the business he was bred to, having been a tallow chandler, has made several of his relatives very happy here at Hendred and elsewhere, by the good legacies he has left them; his name was Greening: he was brother to one of my parish, to whose children he has been very kind; one of his nieces, who had lived with him about two years since the death of his wife, has £50 per annum and a legacy of £1,000 besides all his plate and furniture; two other nieces £1,000 a piece; four children of another niece £200 a piece, to his nephew the son of my parishioner, who was bred up by him in his own business £500; to another niece who is married to a publican at Wantage £500, besides a bond of £850, that he has given up, being money lent for the purchase of the house she and her husband have lately bought; to his brother here at Hendred and his wife, who are an old and feeble couple, and keep a small school for children, £200, which I could wish had been rather more, so as to have made the remainder of their lives a little more comfortable; for they have lived well in their time: but I hope that daughter now at Molesey, who is a single woman, will consider her aged parents, and be a comfort to them, by making some small addition to their present income: Molly Shepherd I believe knows the family; and I reckon it will be her opinion, as well as my own and every one's else, that Mrs. Hester Greening (who is the niece now at Molesey) will not be very long without a partner to share her good fortune, as she always was a spruce dressing lass, and seemed not averse to the pleasures of a double bed.

I reckon you may have seen by the papers, that Dr. Spry of the Commons is married to a Miss Pitt; I think he has played his cards well, for the Archdeacon tells us that her fortune is £5,000 and secured to her and her children in Chancery; her father who is lately dead, was elder brother to the great Mr. Pitt, and a man of very good estate; he left a son who is not returned from his travels, and another daughter, who was married some-time ago to a gentleman of very great fortune, but makes her a little unhappy by being very covetous: Mr. Pitt had some incumbrances upon his estate some years ago, which obliged him to live in Holland, till all things were settled and brought to rights; and it was then I suppose that this fortune was secured in the manner I have mentioned; here it was that Dr. Spry's negotiations with the young lady first commenced, being at Utrecht with Lord Glenorchy, and acquainted with Mr. Pitt and his family: this you may judge is no small joy to the Archdeacon and all the family, who cannot but be well pleased with an alliance so judiciously made by this able civilian: I am heartily glad of it, for he is a very deserving man; and at the same time I am glad, that the Archdeacon, now in the decline of his life, has such frequent earnests given to him, of the future welfare of all his family; for all his sons now I think are in a fair way of doing well, the youngest, who was born the first year I came to Hendred, being lately entered at Oxford, and made Postmaster of Merton, of about £20 a year, as the next above him was in the summer made a Fellow of the same college, worth to him better than £50 a year; a charming prospect for the good old man!

P.S. Poor Sir John! I am sorry to hear the account you give: he must yield at last, I am afraid; and that too before it's long.

Dec. 22d. 1761

Dear Sir,

Had I kept my last letter a post longer, I should have given you an account of a birth we have had in our family, for in the afternoon of that day, in which my letter went away, Sarah was taken bad, so as not to be able to be removed; and after a bustle for some hours, she was safely delivered of a fine lusty boy, about two the next morning; it was quite unexpected, for she did not think of any such alteration in her, till the latter end of this month, and had provided every thing against that time: but she has continued very well ever since, and has had a very good sort of a woman, who has been her nurse, and done her business at the same time; and as she has been provided with every thing for her use, at her husband's expense, we have not found that inconvenience in it, which might have been expected; for as her nurse has done what she otherwise would have done herself, we have only missed the sight of her below stairs for a fortnight; for she came down last Sunday, and does her business about the house as usual, and sometime this week the nurse goes off with the child, which is the quietest thing that ever was, for it is very seldom we hear it cry: we think it has happened very luckily much better than if she had stayed as long as she had expected; for now she is able to get us some minced pies, and do what we have to do at Christmas. The child's name is Joe, and is to be dry nursed. You say, that my sisters tell you nothing of their concerns; and indeed I much question whether we should have known so much, unless I had asked them particularly about them, when I was last with them; for in none of their letters have they ever said, where my mother was buried, or in what manner, which is a circumstance one would naturally have expected from them; that she was buried at Downe I conclude, because upon my asking them that question they told me, it was her own desire; but with regard to the manner of it, we know nothing: we had desired to know, whether they should continue at Downe, or where they intended to dispose of themselves; in answer to this, we are informed, that they leave Downe either today or tomorrow, and are to live at Ilford in Essex, where they have taken a house. I am afraid the old furniture will not be the better, for the journeys it has taken so lately. My brother Tom has been at Downe, before my mother died, but what steps he has taken since, with regard to little Becky I know not; I expect to see him here soon after Christmas, and then I shall talk to him. I am glad to hear there is so good harmony again between Sir John and his brother, and likewise that business at Seaford is over to the advantage of Mr. Peachey; for I was a little afraid, we should lose all our franks. My young spark came home last Saturday with his nails in his old shoes, but as there is yet no occasion for them, I have given him proper instructions how he is to use them, when the frost comes, as I apprehend from the accounts we have from abroad, that we in England shall have our share of hard weather. I am very glad to hear you continue on the mending line, and hope you will have no returns of your disorder. Our neighbour the Archdeacon is returned to Cuddesden, a house near Oxford of his brother the Bishop, it being thought advisable on account of the air: he has his new daughter and her husband Dr. Spry, with him there, who is a niece of the great Mr. Pitt's, his elder brother's daughter, and a fortune of £5,000, so it will make a pretty addition to the Doctor's Commons.

East Hendred Church from the south-east

(S.A. Davies)

[From Albinia Woodward to Mrs London]                    Janry 20 1753
Dear Madam,

I received yours yesterday in the evening, but that was too late to prevent
Molly Shepard's going to Reading, for she come here on Wednesday, and
set out Friday morning for Reading, as that is the day the higler goes from
here and returns on Saturdays; she thought of going to London as today,
but not to go to my mother's till Sunday or Monday, time enough to
prevent her sending to the Inn, as she had an acquaintance would meet her
there on Saturday; we had no possibility of sending after her, but had I
known before you hadn't wanted her so soon, she should have stayed here
till next Friday, which would have been time enough for her to have gone;
but as it has happened so, hope you Madam will not be uneasy at her being
some days longer than was designed at my Mother Woodward's as I dare
say she will not be so her self for (as you observe) she is always very ready
to serve her friends in any thing that is in her power, and as Molly will be
longer with her dont doubt but she will find something to employ her whilst
she is there and not let her idle away her time which might not be for her
good: Mr. Woodward writes to my Mother today, to let her know how this
affair stands, and I thought proper to give you as early notice of her being
gone from here as I could, because if you had any orders to send to her in
Town.
 I am very glad to hear your health is mended since we heard last, and
that you found your grandson and all well at Mrs. Crofts. I know of no
reason to think of our family being any larger than it is at present, so hope
we shall keep these we have, & not have any more; we are all very well, only
Mr. Woodward's eyes have been a little out of order again, since the frost
returned. We have lately had a piece of news which, as it concerns a Family
that we had always great reason to respect, gives us a good deal of concern:
you perhaps Madam may have heard us speak of Mr. Wymondsole, who has
3 sons, and only one of them married to a very fine lady, upon whom alone
depended the continuation of the family; they have all for some time been
very solicitous for an heir, but though she has several times been with child,
and once had one lived about a week, their expectations have still been
frustrated; but it is happy for them all, that she has had none live; for an
intrigue has lately been discover'd, between her and a brother of Lord Til .
. . ys, they being taken in bed together, & a divorce is now suing out; for it
had been an unhappy thing to have had children that perhaps were none of
ye Husband's: we are extremely sorry for the old gentleman and his sons,
who must certainly be under great afflictions, as they always showed the
greatest love and respect to her that can be imagined. This story has taken
up more of my paper, than I was aware of, & Mr. Woodward designs

writing a line, to my uncle, so must conclude with duty to your self and my
uncle & am

Dear Madam
Your Obedient niece
& Humble Servant
Albinia Woodward

April 19, 1755

Dear Madam,

I am much obliged to you for your letter, and always think my self so, when
ever you do me the favour to write to me; though I have many other
obligations to make my acknowledgements for, particularly your's and my
uncle's many civilities to my good gentleman, and kind presents to my self
and little girl. I don't doubt, but the ladies in Axyard did their utmost, to
make their house agreeable to you, and believe they were really much
pleased with having your company there; I understand Mrs. Croft's little
one being so long before it made its appearance, gave them that pleasure
something longer than you at first intended; I desire you and Mrs. Croft, to
accept of my congratulations upon her own safety, and the arrival of the
little stranger. We were much concerned to find by my uncle's last letter,
that the complaint he had when Mr. Woodward was with you, had not yet
left him; and the more so, that it is of such a nature, as deprives him of his
chief amusements of reading and writing; and really quitting such an old
companion as one's snuff box, to those that have used themselves to it, is no
small denial, but I hope the amendment in the weather will have a good
effect upon him; and if you Madam and he will give me leave, I think I can
prescribe a remedy that would be of service to him, and that is taking a
journey; and I have the more confidence in it, as I think travelling so much,
(though even in bad weather) has mended my gentleman's health, but as no
physicians prescribe without a fee, I hope to be a gainer by it, and that his
journey may be to Hendred, where yours and his company will give a great
deal of pleasure; and if you Madam would join your interest in persuading
him to it, I do really think it would do him good.

We had every bed in our house in use last week (though a very bad time
of the year for provisions but will soon mend,) my youngest brother (the
same that was in Town) was here, and we have had the long talked of visit
from my cousin and his tutor; he has promised a visit from Oxford this four
year, that he has been there; he leaves the University this summer, how he
is to be disposed of next, he said he didn't know, whether to travel or stay at
home; he is a modest, sensible young man, and seems very happy in his
tutor, who is a mighty well bred (and said to be a very learned) man, and
there is the appearance of great friendship between them.

I think by their account of Mr. Longford, and what you mention in your letter, Miss Sergison has disposed of herself and money to a direct sot, for Mr. Campion told a remarkable instance of his love for his bottle; that when he appeared as a bridegroom, he engaged his sister to dance with him, but the lady was forced to sit still, for the gentleman could not keep upon his legs. I have already made my letter long enough to tire you, will not add any more to it, but mine and my young one's duty to your self and my uncle, and that I am

Dear Madam,
Your Obedient Niece
and Humble Servant
Albinia Woodward

# Stock List

**Avalon and Sedgemoor.** Desmond Hawkins.
ISBN 0 86299 016 5. 192pp illustrated. 219mm × 157mm.
£4.50, $9.50. *Paper edition only.*

**Along the Great North and Other Roads,**
The North Road Cycling Club 1885–1980. A.B. Smith.
ISBN 904387 73 9. 192pp. 219mm × 157mm. £6.95, $15.75

**Canonical Houses of Wells.** Sherwin Bailey.
ISBN 0 904387 91 7. 192pp. 215mm × 138mm.
£8.95, $18.75.

**In Chimley Corner.** Jan Stewer. Rpr. 1927.ISBN
0 904387 56 9. 256pp. 196mm × 127mm £4.95. $11.25

**Chronicles of London.** C.L. Kingsford. Rpr. 1905.
ISBN 0 904387 15 1. x.viii + 368pp. 216mm × 138mm.
£14.00. Not available from Humanities Press.

**The Civil War in Worcestershire, 1642-1646; and the
Scotch Invasion of 1651.** J.W. Willis-Bund. Rpr. 1905,
ISBN 0 904387 32 1. vi + 268p. 4pp illus. 3pp maps.
216mm × 138mm. £6.95, $15.75.

**The Complete Peerage.** George Edward Cockayne et al.
ISBN 0 904387 82 8. 6 vols. Photoreduced 4pp to view
472pp, 584pp, 408pp, 496pp, 448pp, 416pp.
248mm × 172mm. £300.00, $675.00.

**Concerning Agnes.** Desmond Hawkins.
ISBN 0 904387 97 6. 160pp illustrated. 235mm × 155mm.
£7.95, $16.75.

**Cotswold Churches.** David Verey. ISBN 0 904387 78 X.
192pp illustrated. 219mm × 157mm. £3.95, $9.00.
*Paper edition only.*

**A Cotteswold Manor, being the History of Painswick.**
Welbore St. Clair Baddeley. Rpr. 1929. N. Intro.
Geoffrey Saunders. ISBN 0 904387 54 2. xiv + 262pp.
42pp ilus. 219mm 157mm. £12.00, $27.00.

**The Crown and Local Communities** in England and
France in the Fifteenth Century. Ed. J.R.L. Highfield &
Robin Jeffs. ISBN 0 904387 67 4. 192pp. 219mm × 157mm.
£8.95, $11.25. *Paper* ISBN 0 904387 79 8. £4.95, $11.25

**The Diary of a Cotswold Parson.** Revd. F.E. Witts,
1783-1854. Ed. David Verey. ISBN 0 904387 19 4.
192pp illustrated. 216mm × 138mm. £7.95, $19.25.
*Paper* ISBN 0 904387 33 X. £3.95, $8.00.

**The Diary of a Pilgrimage.** Jerome K. Jerome.
ISBN 0 86299 010 6. 160pp illustrated. 192mm × 127mm.
£1.95, $4.25. *Paper edition only.*

**The Diary of a Rowing Tour** from Oxford to London in
1875. Howard Williams. ISBN 0 904387 69 0.
168pp illustrated. 219mm × 157mm. £7.95, $16.75.
*Paper* ISBN 0 904387 74 4. £3.95, $8.25.

**Dursley and Cam.** David E. Evans. ISBN 0 904387 88 7.
128pp illustrated. 219mm × 157mm. £3.95, $8.25.
*Paper edition only.*

**The English Landscape Garden.** H.F. Clark. Rpr. 1948.
ISBN 0 904387 38 0. 96pp + 32pp illus.
248mm × 172mm. £6.00, $16.50.

**Evergreens and Other Short Stories.** Jerome K. Jerome.
ISBN 0 86299 011 4. 112pp illustrated 192mm × 124mm.
£1.50, $3.25.

**Excellent Cassandra.** Joan Johnson. ISBN 0 904387 76 3.
160pp illustrated. 219mm × 157mm. £7.95, $18.00.

**False, Fleeting, Perjur'd Clarence, George, Duke of
Clarence 1449–78.** Michael Hicks. ISBN 0 904387 44 5.
270pp. 8pp illus. 216mm × 138mm. £8.95, $20.00.

**Frederick III,** German Emperor 1888. John Van der Kiste.
ISBN 0 904387 77 1. 244pp illustrated. 219mm × 157mm.
£8.95, $20.25.

**George Thorpe and the Berkeley Company.**
Eric Gethyn-Jones. ISBN 0 904387 83 6. 296pp
illustrated. 219mm × 157mm. £7.95, $18.00.

**Gloucester Cathedral.** David Verey & David Welander.
ISBN 0 904387 40 2. £6.95, $15.75. 160pp illustrated.
219mm × 157mm. *Paper* ISBN 0 904387 34 8. £3.95, $8.00.

**Gloucestershire Churches.** David Verey. ISBN 0 904387
78 X. 192pp illustrated (32pp full colour).
245mm × 169mm. £2.95, $6.75. *Paper edition only.*

**A Handful of History.** J.R.S. Whiting.
ISBN 0 86299 0002 9. vi + 201pp illustrated.
230mm × 154mm. £4.25, $9.00.

**Historical Records of Bisley with Lypiatt.**
Mary A. Rudd. Rpr. 1937. N. Intro. Geoffrey Sanders.
ISBN 0 904387 16 X. xii + 438pp. 16pp illus.
216mm × 138mm. £11.00, $24.75.

**A History of Cheltenham.** Gwen Hart.
ISBN 0 904387 87 9. 350pp illustrated (col. frontis.).
219mm × 157mm. £12.50, $26.25.

**History of Cirencester, The Roman Corinium.**
K.J. Beecham. Rpr. 1887 + additions booklet 1910. N.
Intro. David Verey. ISBN 0 904387 18 6. vi + 314 +
30pp illustrated. 200mm × 235mm. £11.00, $24.75.

**A History of Malvern.** Brian S. Smith.
ISBN 0 904387 31 3. x + 310pp illustrated.
216mm × 138mm. £6.50, $14.75.

**The History of King Richard the Third.**
Sir George Buck. Ed. A.N. Kincaid. ISBN 0 904387 26 7.
cxlvi + 362pp. 225mm × 172mm. £30.00, $60.50.
*Paper* ISBN 0 86299 008 4. £16.00, $34.00.

**A History of Tetbury.** Eric Hodgson.
ISBN 0 904387 10 0. 136pp. 32pp illus.
216mm × 138mm. £6.95, $15.75.

**A House of Correction.** J.R.S. Whiting.
ISBN 0 904387 27 5. 124pp illustrated.
216mm × 138mm. £5.50, $12.50.

**Idle Thoughts of an Idle Fellow.** Jerome K. Jerome.
ISBN 0 86299 009 2. 144pp illustrated. 192mm × 124mm.
£1.95, $4.25.

**Illustrated Cheltenham Guide of 1845.** George Rowe.
ISBN 0 904387 95 X. 168pp illustrated. 216mm × 157mm.
£3.95, $8.25. *Paper edition only.*

**The Ingenious Mr. Pedersen.** David E. Evans.
ISBN 0 904387 29 1. 128pp illustrated. 216mm × 138mm.
£4.50, $10.25.

**In Spite of Dungeons.** S.J. Davies. ISBN 0 904387 11 9.
192pp illustrated. 216mm × 138mm. *Paper.* £3.95, $7.50.

**Letters from a Flying Officer.** Rothesay Stuart Wortley.
ISBN 0 86299 17 3. viii + 208pp illustrated.
192mm × 127mm. £3.95, $8.25. *Paper edition only.*

**Lister's — The First Hundred Years.** David E. Evans.
ISBN 0 904387 23 2. 256pp illustrated. 216mm × 138mm.
£6.95, $15.75.

**Men and Armour for Gloucestershire in 1608.**
John Smith. Rpr. 1902. ISBN 0 904387 49 6. xiv + 424pp.
248mm × 172mm. £20.00, $36.00.

**Methodism and the Revolt of the Field.** Nigel Scotland.
ISBN 0 904387 46 1. 296pp illustrated. 219mm × 157mm.
£12.00, $22.50.

**Minchinhampton and Avening.** A.T. Playne. Rpr. 1915.
N. Intro. Geoffrey Sanders. ISBN 0 904387 25 9.
xii + 188pp. 24pp illus. 216mm × 138mm. £9.00, $20.50.

**A Month in England.** H.T. Tuckerman.
ISBN 0 86299 020 3. 156pp illustrated. 192mm × 124mm.
£2.95, $6.25.

**Moonraker County.** Lornie Leete-Hodge.
ISBN 0 904387 92 5. 144pp illustrated. 219mm × 157mm.
£3.95. *Paper edition only.* Not available in U.S.A.

**An Account of the Mutiny on HMS Bounty.**
William Bligh. Ed. Robert Bowman. ISBN 0 904387 47 X.
160pp illustrated. 248mm × 172mm. £8.95, $23.50.
*Paper* ISBN 0 86299 005 X. £4.95, $10.50.

**The Mystery of the Princes.** Audrey Williamson.
ISBN 0 904387 28 3. 216pp. 16pp illus. 216mm × 138mm.
£6.95. *Paper* ISBN 0 904387 48 8. £3.95, $8.25.
Paper edition only available from Humanities Press.

**John Nash and the Village Picturesque.** Nigel Temple.
ISBN 0 904387 24 0. xx + 176pp. 32pp illus.
248mm × 172mm. £15.00, $33.00.
*Paper* ISBN 0 86299 007 6. £5.95, $12.50.

**The Old Gloucester, The Story of a Cattle Breed.**
Adam Stout. ISBN 0 904387 42 9. 96pp. 10pp illus.
3 maps. 216mm × 138mm £4.95, $11.25

**A Parcel of Ol' Crams.** Jan Stewer. Rpr. 1930.
ISBN 0 904387 57 7. 256pp. 196mm × 127mm. £4.95,
$11.25.

**Patronage the Crown and the Provinces** in Later
Medieval England. Ed. Ralph A. Griffiths. ISBN
0 904387 43 3. 192pp. 219mm × 157mm. £7.95, $20.75.

**Patronage Pedigree and Power in Later Medieval
England.** Ed. Charles Ross. ISBN 0 904387 37 2. 224pp.
216mm × 138mm. £7.95. Not available from Humanities
Press.

**Richard III as Duke of Gloucester and King of
England.** Caroline A. Halsted. Rpr. 1844.
ISBN 0 904387 14 3. 2 vols., xii + 458pp, xii + 602pp.
216mm × 138mm. £30.00, $67.50.
*Paper* ISBN 0 904387 41 0. £16.00, $36.00.

**Richard III up to Shakespeare.** George E. Churchill.
Rpr. 1900. ISBN 904387 05 4. 548pp. 216mm. × 138mm.
£12.00. Not available from Humanities Press.

**Roman Gloucestershire.** Alan McWhirr.
ISBN 0 904387 63 1. 192pp illustrated. 219mm × 157mm.
£7.95, $18.00. *Paper* ISBN 0 904387 60 7. £3.95, $9.00.

**Roman Mosaics in Britain.** David Neal.
ISBN 0 904387 64 X. 208pp illustrated. + 4pp full colour.
Volume includes 2 colour microfiche. 297mm × 210mm.
£9.95, $22.50. *Paper edition only.*

**Romano-Lavo-Lil, A Book of the Gypsy.** George Borrow.
ISBN 0 86299 024 6. 192pp. 192mm × 124mm.
£2.95, £6.25.

**The Rous Roll.** John Rous. Rpr. 1859. N. Intro.
Charles Ross. ISBN 0 904387 43 7. xviii + 134pp.
32pp illus. 248mm × 172mm. £12.00, $31.50

**The Rural Economy of Glocestershire.** William Marshall.
Rpr. 1796. ISBN 0 904387 22 4. vols., xxxii + 332pp.,
xxiv + 368pp. 200 × 130mm. £28.00, $54.00. (2 vol. set).

**Somersetshire Delineated.** C. & J. Greenwood. Rpr. 1822.
N. Intro. Robert Dunning. ISBN 0 904387 54 4.
viii + 216pp. 216mm × 138mm. £6.95, $13.50.

**Southern History** volume 3. Ed. J.R. Lowerson.
ISBN 0 904387 65 8. 288pp. 216mm × 138mm. £12.50,
$28.25. *Paper* ISBN 0 904387 66 6. £7.50, $17.00.
Volume 4. Ed. J.R. Lowerson. ISBN 0 904387 93 3.
296pp. 216mm × 138mm. £12.50, $28.25.
*Paper* ISBN 0 904387 94 1. £7.50, $17.00.

**Stow-on-the-Wold.** Joan Johnson. ISBN 0 904387 35 6.
160pp. 19pp illus. 3 maps. 216mm × 138mm. £6.95, $13.50.

**The Stroudwater Canal.** Michael Handford.
ISBN 0 904387 30 5. 337pp. + 32pp illus.
216mm × 138mm. £8.95, $21.25. *Paper* £4.95, $11.25.

**Three Men in a Boat.** Jerome K. Jerome.
ISBN 0 86299 028 9. 240pp illustrated. 192mm × 124mm.
£1.95, $4.25.

**Three Men on the Bummel.** Jerome K. Jerome.
ISBN 0 86299 029 7. 232pp illustrated. 192mm × 124mm.
£1.95, $4.25.

**Under the Hill.** Simon Herrick ISBN 0 904387 36 4.
144pp illustrated. 219mm × 157mm. £4.95, $11.25.

**A Voyage to New Holland.** William Dampier. Ed.
James Spencer. ISBN 904387 75 5. 256pp illustrated.
248mm × 172mm. £9.95, $22.50.

**Wall Painting in Roman Britain.** Norman Davey &
Roger Ling. ISBN 904387 96 8. 232pp illustrated
(+ 8pp full colour). Volume includes 1 colour microfiche.
297mm × 210mm. £11.95, $25.25. *Paper edition only.*

**West Country Gardens.** John Sales. ISBN 0 904387 55 0.
272pp. 15pp illus. 4pp full colour. 13 maps.
216mm × 154mm. £7.95, $18.00.
*Paper* ISBN 0 904387 84 4. £3.95, $8.25.

**West Midland Gardens.** Ron Sidwell.
ISBN 0 904387 71 2. 256pp illustrated (8pp full colour).
219mm × 157mm. £7.95, $18.00.

**White Horses and other Hill Figures.** Morris Marples.
ISBN 0 904387 59 3. 224pp illustrated. 216mm × 138mm.
£3.95, $9.00. *Paper edition only.*

**In a Wiltshire Village.** Scenes from Rural Victorian Life.
Alfred Williams. Ed. Michael J. Davis.
ISBN 0 904387 62 3. 192pp illustrated. 219mm × 157mm.
£3.95, $9.00. *Paper edition only.*

**The Witchcraft and Folklore of Dartmoor.**
Ruth St Leger-Gordon. ISBN 0 86299 021 1. 152pp
illustrated. 219mm × 157mm. £3.95, $9.00.
*Paper edition only.*

**Wotton-under-Edge.** E.S. Lindley. ISBN 0 904387 17 8.
344pp. 16pp illus. 216mm × 138mm. £7.50, $17.00.

**Wotton-under-Edge, A Century of Change.** Ed.
Geoffrey Masefield. ISBN 0 904387 51 8. 112pp.
52pp illus. 219mm × 145mm. £3.95, $9.00.
*Paper edition only*